Buying & Running a Guesthouse or Small Hotel

Thank you for buying one of our books. We hope you'll enjoy the book, and that it will help you start and run your own successful guesthouse or small hotel.

We always try to ensure our books are up to date, but contact details seem to change so quickly that it can be very hard to keep up with them. If you do have any problems contacting any of the organisations listed at the back of the book please get in touch, and either we or the author will do what we can to help. And if you do find correct contact details that differ from those in the book, please let us know so that we can put it right when we reprint.

Please do also give us your feedback so we can go on making books that you want to read. If there's anything you particularly liked about this book – or you have suggestions about how it could be improved in the future – email us on info@howtobooks.co.uk

The Publishers
www.howtobooks.co.uk

If you want to know how...

Start & Run Your Own Business
The complete guide to succeeding with a small business

Book-keeping & Accounting for the Small Business
How to keep the books and maintain financial control over your business

The Ultimate Business Plan
Secure financial backing and support for a successful business

Small Business Tax Guide

howtobooks

Please send for a free copy of the latest catalogue:

How To Books
3 Newtec Place, Magdalen Road,
Oxford OX4 1RE, United Kingdom
email: info@howtobooks.co.uk
http://www.howtobooks.co.uk

Buying & Running a Guesthouse or Small Hotel

Make a fresh start
and run your own
guesthouse

SUCCESSFUL BUSINESS START-UPS

Dan Marshall

howtobooks

Published by How To Books Ltd
3 Newtec Place, Magdalen Road
Oxford OX4 1RE, United Kingdom
Tel: (01865) 793806 Fax: (01865) 248780
info@howtobooks.co.uk
www.howtobooks.co.uk

First published 2003
Reprinted 2005

British Library Cataloguing in Publication Data.
A catalogue record for this book is available from the British Library.

Edited by Barbara Ball
Cover design by Baseline Arts Ltd, Oxford
Produced for How To Books by Deer Park Productions
Typeset by PDQ Typesetting, Newcastle-under-Lyme, Staffs.
Printed and bound in Great Britain by Bell & Bain Ltd, Glasgow

NOTE: The material contained in this book is set out in good faith for general
guidance and no liability can be accepted for loss or expense incurred as a result of
relying in particular circumstances on statements made in the book. Laws and
regulations are complex and liable to change, and readers should check the current
position with the relevant authorities before making personal arrangements.

Contents

List of illustrations

Preface

Most people leave employment to start their own business for a number of reasons. They are generally classified within the headings 'push factors' or 'pull factors'. Push factors include redundancy, being asked to leave the job, lengthy joblessness, simply can't get along with the boss/colleagues etc, while pull factors include finally making up your mind to do what you always wanted to do. In the back of your mind you are thinking, 'Yippee! I'll be my own boss at last.' Maybe, but maybe not!

Whatever the reason, there comes the time when you and possibly your spouse/partner are looking seriously at the prospect of having your own business and in this case, a guesthouse or small hotel. At this point, there are many factors to be considered. Ask yourself some questions.

Is my experience relevant to running a guesthouse or small hotel?

It may be that you have expertise that is beneficial to operating a guesthouse or hotel but does not address the core needs of the business. Perhaps you are a computer expert, and while this is helpful, it does not help with the core 'hospitality' tasks.

If you do not have experience of the industry, it would be beneficial to take a position in a small hotel, ideally as a general assistant to the owners. In doing this, you will be working in every area and gaining invaluable experience, some of it while making mistakes at your employer's expense!

Most importantly, this will enable you to be sure that you can deal with guests on a daily basis with a necessary, friendly style. In addition, it will make you realise that this lifestyle means that you spend many hours on your feet. It is physically tiring, although in time, you will become fitter and more able to withstand this physical aspect of the business. In a later chapter, I will help you to 'use your brain to save your legs!'

If you truly enjoy this experience, you will have started on a learning curve which will help in making the decision to progress to the next step – and this at someone else's cost rather than your own.

Do I enjoy dealing with people?

When you analyse what you are good at, consider how these various attributes relate to running a guesthouse. Some will be there but some will not. It is vital that you consider not only how well you deal with people (paying guests), but also whether you have the patience and attitude to deal with the more awkward ones. Remember, you will be spending many hours of the day with guests and possibly staff so 'people skills' are vital. In addition, spending many working hours a day with your spouse/partner may present some unexpected relationship problems.

What other skills do I need?

In the case of a husband and wife team, it would be helpful if at least one has certain skills which would be useful for the operation of the guesthouse or hotel.

◆ **Cooking skills** While this depends on the extent to which you want to develop the business, minimal skills will be required to provide a first class breakfast, while a more complex situation is the provision of dinner and possibly lunch. More on this in the chapter on Food and Beverage.

◆ **Housekeeping and cleanliness skills** This area, while mundane, is vitally important since guests readily accept sleeping in a bed someone else slept in the night before only if there is no evidence of the previous occupant. The guest room and bathroom must be 'as new'. Everything must be fresh: no hairs in the bath, no toothpaste marks on the sink, etc. Thorough and professional housekeeping is vital and this will be covered in Chapter 7, Housekeeping Operations.

◆ **Reservations, reception and billing skills** This is not a complex area but it must be an accurate one. Not having a room for a booked guest is a terrible failing. It is, however, one which can be easily avoided with a reliable system. Similarly, ensuring the guest account is accurate takes good recording skills but is not complex. More of this in the chapter on Reservations and Reception.

◆ **Service skills** Someone will be involved in serving both food and drinks and possibly wine. Training may well be required and this should be considered by the member of the team who will not usually be involved in the kitchen activities. This may be gained during the pre-purchase 'internship' while working for someone else.

◆ **Being organised** This area will be covered in every chapter and it is vital that each person has routines and work duties which coincide with and complement the other partner's routines. This will be explained in more detail later and will show the need to be able to manage a number of tasks at the same time.

How much money can I invest?

I hope to help you to make a decision on which property you might wish to purchase. There are many possible options, however, vital to this decision is the amount of money you will be able to invest.

◆ How much cash is available?
◆ Is this dependent on the sale of another property?
◆ Does it mean borrowing from a friend or family?

If you have enough money to buy a property outright, that is wonderful. What you must try to avoid is a situation where you are working long hours only to pay interest on a loan with the prospect of paying off the loan in the far distant future. These issues will be discussed in the first chapter.

What do I want from the business in terms of financial return?

In a small business such as a guesthouse or a small hotel, the chances of making a huge amount of money are slim. There is a limit to the volume of business the property and you can handle. The trade off is the 'life-style' aspect of the business which relates to you working in your home and having the costs of your home included in the business costs. (There are taxation implications here however which must be considered.) Depending on the location of the business, it may well be seasonal, meaning that you work hard for a period of time but have time off for a period of time, albeit, without income. This is generally countered by the fact that you have not had time to spend money during the busy period!

Another consideration however, is that there is the likely growth in the value of the property, provided you are maintaining it well, as well as the increased goodwill element of the business if you are doing a good job.

Running a guesthouse is a 'life-style' business. What you are doing is using your home, to make a living. You are inviting people into your home, offering them what they want and making a fair and honest charge for what they are receiving. If you can meet and even exceed their expectations, then you have the basis for a stable and growing business while enjoying the comforts of your home and life style.

What this book will do for you is to give information and guidance in a number of areas. The first few chapters will help you to identify the property you wish to operate, leading to pre-opening activities. After this, the following chapters deal with operational issues, including some aspects of food and beverage activities, housekeeping and an insight into simple but useful marketing strategies. In addition, there are pointers and guidance related to maintenance, gardening and property operation. I will stress throughout the book the need for routines and processes, which will help you 'work smart, not hard"

There is an important section on the financial side of the business and how you can keep control of your costs and cash flow. I will recommend you keep statistics, which will help you identify year on year, how you are progressing and help you set targets for the future.

Most importantly, throughout the book, I will keep reminding you that without the goodwill of the guest, your business will have no future. In any business, but particularly, a service business, it is vital to meet the customer's needs, wants and expectations. Of course, if you can exceed them, you will immediately go ahead of the competition.

When all is said and done, in your mind or even on paper, you must have a mission or a set of goals or objectives for this new and exciting venture. Your goals should relate logically to the resources available to you. As you embark on this venture, you will find, possibly as you did in your previous life, that resources are limited and they must be managed effectively to achieve your objectives. By resources I am talking about:

- available cash
- equipment
- the property itself
- staff, if they are to be part of the equation, and the cost of them
- the time you and your spouse/partner have available in any one day as well as the energy you both have.

Perhaps this means that the goals have to be trimmed or modified from that original plan. By the way, my simple formula for planning a mission statement is to write a sentence or two, which answers the questions:

- **Who are we?**
- **What do we do?**
- **Who do we do it for?**
- **How do we do it?**

You might come up with something like '**We are a service minded couple who enjoy making people happy. We offer a quality guesthouse/small hotel and pride ourselves on hospitality, cleanliness and value for money for our guests, who are predominantly retired couples seeking a friendly, comfortable base for exploring the area.**'

This then, becomes your vision of what you hope to achieve and from time to time, you may wish to re-read this statement to check that it is still appropriate and also to see if you are indeed achieving what you intended to achieve.

This book then will lead from your thoughts of buying a guesthouse or small hotel through the decision making process, the start-up and then the ongoing operation. I will use my experience of hotel and restaurant operation to assist you in deciding what level of business you wish to operate and then, help you to set your standard at that level. This standard will be one, which inevitably, must meet your guests' needs, wants and expectations and should be one that you can achieve comfortably.

Dan Marshall

For

Georgina Storie Marshall

Who would have been proud.

For Sheila, who creates quality in our business

and for

Tiffany Irene Lema

and

Jessie Ann Marshall.

CHAPTER ONE

Substantiating the Dream

Is this a pipedream or are you really committed to buying and running a guesthouse or small hotel? This chapter will help you to decide. A short exercise will give you the opportunity to analyse your present situation and to examine the move you are contemplating. If, after this, you still feel convinced that this is the way forward, you will learn about possible methods of raising the necessary finances and from that, you will be presented with a format for making an approach to a lender. Many experts will support you as you embark on this journey, and this chapter will introduce you to them and will give some information regarding working with them to achieve your goals.

Characteristics of the small business owner

Most people who write about small businesses try to define the qualities needed to be a successful small business owner. Such research has identified the successful owner as being ambitious, pragmatic, emotionally stable, healthy, skilful in solving problems, energetic, liking the responsibility of the business, able to see detail within the 'big' picture, and self-confident. Do not panic here since it is unlikely that any one person fits this bill, but if it sounds a bit like you, well and good!

Some questions to ask yourself at this stage might be:

- What are my expectations from this business?
- What skills do I bring to it?
- How confident am I?
- Do I get on well with people?
- Am I prepared to work long hours?
- Am I patient enough to wait for the results I hope to achieve?
- Am I in good health and fit for this kind of physical work?

- How will I handle things if it is not going too well?
- Have I worked with my partner before and is this feasible?

Having thought about your answers, read on and be analytical, but stay positive.

Myths exposed

For most people, the thought of owning one's own business is alluring and tends to be associated with all the trappings of the rich lifestyle: the ideal car; expensive vacations; designer clothes; mixing with the rich and famous, etc. It is not surprising, therefore, that it seems desirable. Can it really be like this? In short, it is hardly likely at all. There are other dreams also associated with having your own business, which should be examined:

- **You are probably dreaming if you think you are likely to become very rich.** As mentioned in the preface, this type of business is not about becoming hugely rich, but more about having a certain lifestyle which is perhaps more acceptable than the 'rat race' of corporate life.

- **You are dreaming if you think you will be your own boss.** Other bosses seem to develop, e.g. the bank you are borrowing from; your spouse/partner; your suppliers, and even your customers or guests.

- **You are dreaming if you think you have nothing to lose.** You can lose the original stake you put into the business if it is unsuccessful. You can lose the confidence of your backers and you can lose confidence in yourself.

- **You are dreaming if you think you can start up without capital.** While it may not be necessary to have all the purchase price of the property, there is a minimal amount, which is required to make the business viable. Most small business failure comes from lack of adequate starting capital. This is discussed later in this chapter in the bank manager section.

Do you really want to do this?

At this stage, it is wise to begin to explore whether this is a pipedream or something you really want to do. How good or bad is your present situation? How good might this alternative really be? Will it truly fulfil you, or will you be back where you started in a couple of years?

It is best to approach this question in an analytical way. To begin the exercise, consider the positives and negatives of your present situation. Following that, try to visualise realistically the positives and negatives of the future situation and then draw some conclusions.

I have started the exercise below by putting in some possible entries.

Positive and negative aspects of your present position

Positive	Negative
Regular income	Perhaps repetitive boredom
Relatively fixed hours	Maybe long hours
Weekend breaks	Need to work unpaid at weekends
Pension scheme (employer contributes)	Managerial stress
Camaraderie of colleagues	Company 'politics'
Perks (possibly company car etc.)	Lack of appreciation
Paid holidays	Lack of ability to make significant change
	Commuting to work

Positive and negative aspects of taking a guesthouse/small hotel

Positive	Negative
No company politics	Long working hours (assumes no staff)
No 'big company' stress	No days off (during season if seasonal)
Giving service and making people happy	Holidays in winter season
Being appreciated for doing a good job	Holidays without income
Making a good living	No income when closed
Long, well-earned holidays! (seasonal)	Lack of privacy
Control and ability to make improvement	Lack of social life
No commuting to work	Always on call

Figure 1.1. Looking at the positives and negatives.

Develop and personalise this chart to obtain a realistic view of where you stand in relation to what you have now and what the future might hold for you.

Having gone through the exercise with your spouse/partner, consider your conclusions. Hopefully, you are now convinced that you are on the right road, so let us consider some other issues.

Common reasons for business failures

The following are some of the reasons why business fail:

- **Inadequate finance**. Many businesses start with inadequate finance and the consequential pressure on the owners detract from their enjoyment of running the business, and can be frustrating and depressing. You need to avoid this problem or the dream might die at an early stage.

- **Borrowing too much.** If you borrow too much, you are simply working for the lender. Borrowing is likely to be at a rate of around two per cent above base rate, so you can calculate your monthly interest payments and check if the business can pay this amount and more, in order to make capital repayments. Many people fail because their interest and capital repayments simply cannot be met. Consider also the frustration of working long and hard, yet having no money left because of the cost of borrowing.

- **Faulty pricing**. Some operators make the mistake of trying to beat the competition by undercutting them and hoping for the best. Their expenses are likely to be similar to yours and if they need that level of income, it is likely that you will also. I will give some guidance on setting prices in Chapter 8.

- **Partnership problems**. These can occur for a number of reasons. One partner may simply not enjoy the life and want to get out. If this is a spouse or partner, then some serious decisions have to be made. If this is a 'sleeping' partner who has helped with the finance, but has no active role in the business, this may result in you trying to buy that person out, leaving you with the 'borrowing too much' problem.

- **Poor control**. This will be addressed in subsequent chapters. However, in simple terms, it is important to be aware of purchase prices for foodstuffs, cleaning materials, equipment and repairs and maintenance. Obtaining quotes for major projects will show hugely varying prices, proving the worth of using this technique. Control of utilities must be addressed, and energy-saving tips will be given in Chapter 10. Maintaining records is important and, depending on the level of business, calculating food and liquor cost percentages on a periodic basis will identify profitability and potential problem areas. More on this topic in Chapter 6.

◆ **Excessive overheads**. It is important to control overhead costs and particularly, the expensive ones. Staffing can be one of the most expensive overheads. Think long and hard before making the decision to hire staff and if you do, you must be careful to have them only when the level of business justifies it. Small business operators sometimes keep staff on board when they are not necessary. They may do so just for company or because they are embarrassed to ask them not to come in. On hiring, explain the process to the employees and only have them at work when their presence is justified by the level of business.

◆ **Poor trading levels**. Before making the purchase, it is necessary to analyse the sales trend and also the potential for increasing the business. The SWOT analysis and the preparation of the business plan which follows will describe this in more detail. If you do not achieve enough business to cover your fixed costs, then the business is not financially viable.

◆ **Drawing cash excessively**. This is a practice sometimes carried out by inexperienced operators who see cash coming in and feel that it belongs to them and is there for their use. The cash that is coming in has to be used to pay the bills, and only the remaining cash after all bills, including tax, is paid, is available to the owners. In this respect, try to look at the business as though it belongs to someone else and you are a paid employee.

Minimising new business risks

To minimise the risk involved in starting a new business, you should:

◆ **Gain relevant experience**. As described in the preface, it makes very good sense to gain some experience of the hospitality industry by working for someone else. If you already have experience, then gain some experience in the areas with which you are not familiar. For example, if you are already a chef, gain experience in housekeeping and in bookkeeping or, at least, take a course.

♦ **Gain immediate family support**. Be sure your spouse/partner is as committed as you are and if you have children, identify their contribution and how they will cope when you are busy for many hours of the day. This is particularly important if you have teenagers since they may well be able to make a realistic contribution to the operation of the business. It may be a good life skill for them to be given specific responsibilities on which you can assess them and hopefully, praise and reward them for a job well done.

♦ **Recognise and be prepared to accept the downsides**. Look again at the box in this chapter which you developed, to identify the negative aspects of taking on this business. Accept that they exist and, with your partner, discuss how you will cope with these aspects of the business. Recognise that this life will mean physically hard work, which of course, will be tempered with the enjoyable association you have with your guests and the constant positive feedback you have from them when you are doing a good job.

♦ **Prepare a business plan**. Even if you do not need to borrow money for the purchase, go through the mental exercise of preparing a business plan so that you become intimately familiar with your business. As you will see from the following sections, the business plan is an important tool for you and for potential lenders.

Finding the cash

Many small business operators start their business with limited capital and sadly, such businesses frequently fail because of this. Even if they just manage to keep their heads above water, they become disillusioned when all the fruits of their labour seem to go to the lender.

The successful operator will have a considerable financial stake in the business and will try to limit borrowing as much as possible. There are a number of possibilities for borrowing money in order to finance the business:

◆ **Borrowing from friends or family**. While this might seem like a good idea and certainly might help you to make the step, it is not without its problems. Sometimes the family member who theoretically, should be the 'sleeping partner' does not take the sleeping role. This person feels that the business is theirs and treats it as such, possibly making use of rooms that could be sold, expecting meals and drinks without payment, etc. If this route to financing is used, strict 'rules' should be agreed at an early stage. In addition, agree that the operator has first choice of alternatively financing the loan if the 'sleeping partner' wants out of the business.

◆ **The bank**. I obtained the following information from my own bank and it is reasonable to assume that all of the major banks lend using similar procedures. My experience is that banks want to see a considerable financial commitment from the operator, however generally they will lend 50 per cent and in some cases, will stretch their involvement to 70 per cent. A variety of products can be made available by a bank and these include such things as:

– **Term loan**. This may be medium or long-term finance to get the business going or to develop it. Interest rates can generally be negotiated and can be variable or fixed.

– **Overdraft**. The effect of this is to provide working capital. This is normally for a fixed period, which may be extended. There is usually a setting up fee and the interest rate is usually negotiable.

– **Business commercial mortgage**. This is a typical mortgage on property and/or land, and the bank would have first charge on the property in case of default. The interest rate is usually negotiable.

– **Asset finance**. This usually relates to funding equipment and vehicles, and options include contract hire, hire purchase and leasing.

– **Small firms loan guarantee scheme**. This type of loan can provide for your working capital or capital expenditure requirement. Such a loan can be made when ordinary bank funding may not be available due to lack of security. Loans may be up to £250,000 with up to ten years to pay. This is a government scheme and usually security is not required. There is a guarantee of part payment in the event of your default.

The business plan

It may be that you have no need to borrow money for your purchase or perhaps you only need a small loan, so it is possible you do not feel the need to prepare a business plan. I strongly recommend, however, that you go through the process, for a number of reasons.

Firstly, it causes you to write down your ideas for the business and enables you to make mistakes only on paper. You also have a record of what you are thinking about. As the plan develops and you go through the various steps, aspects of your previously internalised plan may then seem less than viable as you develop the detail on paper. Perhaps as you investigate further, you may realise that local competition that you thought was unimportant, may well be very strong competition for you. You may also see that the prices you envisaged charging may not provide a profit or be sufficient to repay the interest and capital repayments.

Secondly, as you prepare the plan, you become intimately involved with vital aspects of the business and your confidence builds as you get to know it well. This intimate knowledge of the business may well compensate for some lack of experience since your objectives and expectations become very clear to you. At some point, you may have to make an oral presentation to the potential lender. Your creation of the plan gives you a thorough knowledge of all aspects of the business and you are more likely to be able to stand up and sell it.

In addition, the plan will tell you how much money is needed, when and for how long so that when you visit lenders, you are clear in your mind what your needs are.

A well-prepared business plan will stand you in good stead when making an application for a loan from a bank or other lending institution.

It is possible to buy computer software, which takes you through some of the basic steps of setting up a business plan and you may wish to take this route. Some of the banks provide such software in the form of a CD to help you prepare the plan. If a presentation to a lender is required, this prepared plan helps give a very professional presentation.

The following gives a fairly comprehensive insight into the preparation of a business plan. However you should be aware that there are some key issues that lenders will focus on when they read your plan:

◆ **Security of the asset**. They will want to know that you have a sizeable financial stake in your business and that they have an almost certain chance of getting their money back.

◆ **Customer needs**. They will want to know that you are not simply excited about your idea, but that you have truly recognised your customers' needs, wants and expectations and that your plan shows how they will be met.

◆ **Existence of a market**. They will want to know that there is a good reason why people will stay with you and they will want to know how you will reach this target market.

Executive summary

The presentation of the business plan therefore is important and there are some issues that the lender is most interested in. Every business plan should have an executive summary, which essentially presents, on one page, the gist of the business plan. Busy people may or may not want to read your fine detail, so the executive summary gives them a synopsis, which might offer enough for them to make a decision. This is generally the inside front page of the plan.

Key elements of the business plan

History of the business

In this section of the plan, you will be informing the reader of what went on in the past and you should give a factual description based on what you know of the business as well as details regarding accounts and actual profitability. You should identify positive and negative aspects so that later you can show how you plan to build on the positive and eliminate or change the negative. Brochures and any collateral materials relating to the business will be useful items to present to enhance this section. Consider that you are selling the business as you would to a potential guest.

Shareholders and operators

The lender will be interested to know what the operators bring to the business and their relevant experience. If there are other 'shareholders' or 'sleeping partners' they will want to know what involvement they might have and also whether they are able to pull their investment out of the business easily, causing a problem for the operator. This section can be enhanced by the attachment of a curriculum vitae, provided it is relevant to the operation of a guest house/small hotel. In this section, you are selling to the lender the fact that you are capable of operating and developing the business and being successful.

The business product and/or service

It is important in this section to describe your idea of what the business is offering the guests, with a reasoned explanation of why they will choose this business rather than another one. Some detail relating to the rooms, food available, wine list and other products or services you plan to offer should be included in this section. Any plans for future development can be outlined here. The lender will be interested to see that your business idea is relevant to the needs of the potential customers.

> **I have seen many businesses go to the wall very quickly because the operator tried to force a product on guests who simply did not want it and who did not return. Example: Trying to force a gourmet, à la carte restaurant on guests who want 'cheap and cheerful'.**

The local market and competition

This would include a description of the local area including some information you have gained from researching businesses similar to yours in the locality. This research is useful and I recommend you visit the competition and ask for a brochure and possibly ask to see a room. This gives you an idea of what the competition is offering as well as a feel for the ambience and hospitality in rival establishments. In addition, visit the local tourist office and obtain a copy of a brochure on what the local area has to offer. Visit any of the main stationers and buy local guesthouse/B&B/small hotel guides. If you wish to go into detail, create a grid with the establishments to the top and key information down the side and add the attributes each establishment has, to see which might be similar to what you offer and therefore might be your main competition. Put your establishment in as one of the columns and honestly, begin the comparative process.

   This then is a sample and you can develop it much further, taking into account some aesthetic issues you observed or felt during your visit, such as hospitality, ambiance, comfort and interest. This information will lead you logically to the next section which introduces the SWOT analysis which will assist you in establishing objectives for your business.

	Royal Hotel	Argyll House	Beach House	Westover
Rooms	6	8	4	6
En-suites	4	8	2	6
Lounge	Yes	Yes	No	Yes
Full breakfast	Yes	Yes	Yes	Yes
Dinner	No	Yes	No	Yes
Licence	No	Yes	No	Yes
Wine list	No	Minimal	No	Extensive
Stairs to room	Yes	Yes	No	No
Parking	4 cars	6 cars	4 cars	6 cars
Gardens	Small	Nice	Pretty	Extensive
Pets	Yes	Yes	Yes	No
Children	No	Yes	Yes	Over 10
Credit cards	Yes	Yes	No	No
Cleanliness	Poor	Fair	Good	Very Good

Figure 1.2. Researching the competition.

Establish short term objectives using a SWOT analysis

The SWOT analysis simply means that you consider what are the *opportunities* open to your business, what are the *strengths*, what are the *weaknesses* and what *threatens* your business.

Take a sheet of paper and draw lines to create the sections. Write **Strengths, Weaknesses, Opportunities** and **Threats** in each corner and write under each heading what you believe should go there, e.g. under 'strengths', you might list 'large en-suite bedrooms'. Under 'weaknesses', you might write 'parking for only three cars'. Under 'opportunities', you might write, 'walking tours' (linked with local tour guide). Under 'threats', you might write 'low-cost 80 bedroom hotel proposed for the town three miles away'.

Strengths	Weaknesses
Opportunities	Threats

As these lists are developed, you are digging deep and beginning to identify the positive areas, which you can build on, and the negative issues, which you must plan to resolve in the short term. Some threats, e.g. the new hotel, cannot be changed. However, you can begin to differentiate your property by stressing how big the bedrooms are, and how their décor is homely and consistent with the local area, unlike a standardised large hotel. In discussing the opportunities available, you are showing potential lenders that you have realistic plans to make the venture a success.

The information derived from this exercise becomes the basis of a short-term strategy for the operation and development of the business. If necessary a five-year plan may be developed if it is foreseen that further borrowing may be required as the business develops and possibly expands.

Financial information

It is wise to present previous owners' audited accounts for the past five years if possible and do so year by year on a spreadsheet, so that simple comparisons can be made and trends identified. In Chapter 9, I will suggest a simple profit and loss account format, which can be used for such a presentation. It is important for you to emphasise the trends and show how the business will develop under your management focussing on how you will ideally increase revenues and decrease costs, resulting in acceptable profitability. It is wise to extrapolate at least two years of your profit and loss accounts to show how you expect the business to develop under your management. Lenders will be interested to see that the profitability you predict, takes into consideration any interest charges they might make and a reasonable living for you, the operator.

When preparing budgetary figures, think conservatively rather than excessively optimistically. Do not think 'worst case scenario' but try to be honest and realistic.

Within this section, it will be of interest to include cost control, purchase control and inventory control procedures, as well as cash flow statements and revenue control procedures. Revenue and expense recording systems will be dealt with in Chapter 9, and controls within the food and beverage area will be covered in Chapter 6.

Cash flow analysis

A simple definition of cash flow is 'the movement of cash in and out of the business through the receipt of revenue from guests and the payment for legitimate expenses of the business'.

At the takeover of a business, there are likely to be a number of outgoings, perhaps to pay for stock purchased from the previous owner as well as to pay for advertising charges relating to the future. If the takeover is at a downtime or off-season period, there is likely to be limited revenue or even none at all, and in that case, it is necessary for the new owner to introduce some cash so that cash flow is at least at a balance.

If this is not possible, then an arrangement should be made with the bank, either for a loan or an overdraft facility. For information, there will usually be an arrangement fee for an overdraft, which is around 0.75 per cent of the amount of overdraft facility. In addition, the bank interest on an overdraft is likely to be around two per cent above base rate. For a new business and new account, the bank may offer a small overdraft facility for no set-up fee.

As with the preparation of budgets, I recommend conservatism and realism when preparing the cash flow statement. When preparing the budget, you estimated on a day-by-day, week-by-week basis, what you thought your revenues would be. Revenues in the cash flow statement may be somewhat different if the business is not a 'cash' business.

If your hotel or guesthouse is in a city centre one and deals with accommodation for company representatives, they may well ask to have an account with you, which they will pay on a monthly or longer basis. In other words, although you have put up the guest for three days at the beginning of May, cash may not flow into your bank until the end of June or perhaps later. In some cases, it may never flow in and, if a large proportion of your business is this type of business, then your accountant may suggest you build in a 'bad debts' section of your accounts. Hopefully, this will not happen too often.

The good news on this front is that from the expenses point of view, you may well be able to delay payment to some of your suppliers. It is good business practice to try to stay within the requirements of your suppliers and usually, they will request payment within 30 days of receipt of the goods or service. Remember that if you deal with a cash and carry, they will require cash, possibly cheque or direct debit card for payment. The competitive prices they offer you are predicated on instant flow of cash to them. They want to manage their cash flow as you do.

Another possibility, however, is to have a business credit card for some of your purchases. Usually, the bank will require payment in full of the balance by direct debit. However, this gives you a period of grace before the cash flows out. The benefit also of paying many charges on your credit card means that there are fewer bank charges for the maintenance of your business account.

An abbreviated cash flow statement for three months would look something like the following, showing the flow of cash into the account and out of the account, including the cumulative amount of cash available to the business. Bear in mind that the picture for the low season will be somewhat bleaker as the fixed charges continue at a time when revenue is reduced or non-existent.

	March	April	May
Receipts			
Capital introduced	1,000		
Cash received	2,100	3,200	4,800
Accounts received	150	100	220
Total receipts	3,250	3,300	5,020
Paid out			
Food	320	420	520
Beverages	180	310	340
Insurance	90	90	90
Rates	95	95	95
Heat and light	110	110	140
Wages	0	180	240
Motor expenses	50	60	70
Advertising	120	0	1,740
Miscellaneous	20	50	85
Total paid out	985	1,315	3,320
Net cash flow	2,265	1,985	1,700
Opening balance	0	2,265	4,250
Closing balance	2265	4,250	5,950

Figure 1.3. A typical cash flow statement.

Remember that the only way to improve a negative cash flow situation is either to increase revenue or reduce, or perhaps delay, the payment of expenses. This brings up the subject of marketing and this topic will be dealt with the Chapter 8.

Selecting your support team

There are numerous people you have to deal with external to your business. Some you may choose to deal with, while with others you have no choice. Some are people whose expertise you will use and pay for one way or the other. Others are inevitable to the type of business you will be running, since their role is to keep the public safe.

In the early stage of the process, you will deal with:

◆ estate agents
◆ lawyers
◆ surveyors.

In the next stage, you may deal with:

◆ lawyers
◆ insurance suppliers
◆ bank managers
◆ accountants.

When you are up and running, you will deal with:

◆ accountants
◆ environmental health officers (health inspectors)
◆ health and safety officers
◆ licensing authority officers
◆ the Inland Revenue
◆ fire safety officers
◆ tourist authority and other quality advisors.

A brief introduction to the benefits of working with each of these people follows. However, when it becomes more relevant to a particular section of the book, I will dwell in more detail on the role of a particular advisor.

Estate agents

You should make good use of estate agents as they can help you and save you time and money. However, you must do some homework before approaching them. You need to know what you are looking for. Is it a B&B, a guesthouse or a small hotel? Should it have a bar? Will you serve dinners? Should it be seasonal or year round? Should it require staff or be a two-person operation? You really have to be clear in your mind what you are looking for, although perhaps an element of flexibility may be helpful.

When you have defined the type of property in which you are interested, you will then need to make a decision on the area. Do you want to be in the country; in the city; in a 'manor' house; by the sea; in the mountains? There are so many choices. Seek the services of a specialist hotel agent. Having said that, there are national specialist agencies which deal with hotels/guesthouses, etc. Their advertisements can be found in the national hospitality press magazines, possibly the most prominent one being the *Caterer and Hotelkeeper*, which is a weekly publication. Contact numbers for this magazine are in the Appendix. Some of the national agents are also listed. More on this topic appears in Chapter 2.

When searching for local agents in the areas you have selected, look in the *Yellow Pages* or visit the biggest town in the region and locate the most prominent agency. Look also at the property advertisements in the local press. Meet with the agents to find what they have available. Establish a rapport with the agent and they will try to match your requirements with the available properties in the area. It may well be that through their knowledge of the local area, there are some properties which are not on the market but which might well be approachable.

Do not be surprised if, when you begin to visit some properties, your mind may be changed so that some features, which were important to you before the search, become less important, while others suddenly seem to be a very good idea. When we were looking, we visited several properties, which were on three floors. We then visited one which was all on ground level and we immediately recognised the advantages. This is the one we eventually purchased.

> **Have an open mind and be relatively flexible since no property will exactly meet your criteria, and be careful not to fall in love with one aspect of a property to the extent that you ignore other potential problems.**

Lawyer (solicitor)

In our case, our estate agent was also our lawyer, so when we had found the property, they were able to carry out the conveyance of the purchase. This is not uncommon and the benefit would appear to be that they have experience in the area and know the relevant searches that should be made.

As with the estate agent, it is important that your lawyer knows your aims and objectives so that in all of their dealings with the vendor's lawyer, they keep your interest in the forefront of their activities. It is not uncommon for the lawyer to know other professionals in the area and most likely, they can advise you on the selection of a surveyor, accountant, bank and even insurance brokers. Their local knowledge is usually very useful.

It is normal for the lawyer to make the application on your behalf for a liquor licence. For subsequent renewals however, you can save the lawyer's fee by making the application yourself.

Surveyor

As mentioned above, it is likely that the lawyer will be able to recommend a surveyor. In most areas, there is a representation from the major, multinational surveying companies, but also there will be local ones. Simply put, it may well be that the local company is less expensive than the multinational company. Before selecting a surveyor, be sure that the lending institution will accept a report from that particular surveyor.

Deal directly with the surveyor. As with your lawyer, tell them your aims and objectives. Let them know your experience. Build a rapport. If you have visited the property as a guest without a formal interview with the sellers, explain your feelings and list the things that worry you.

The survey

Generally, if an existing business is being surveyed, the survey will provide information based on the following headings:

The Property	The Business
description	nature of the operation
accommodation	competition
services	existing business
tenure	trade inventory
state of repair	trading records
rating assessment	

In addition, there will probably be an executive summary, which easily identifies key points as well as a section on general remarks. There will be appendices showing location maps, possibly photographs, and trading records as well as valuation definitions to assist in understanding the report. The surveyor will give a valuation of the property and the business. However, it should be noted that market conditions will prevail and if there is considerable interest in the property, it is not to say that a higher bid might be required.

Given that you achieved a personal rapport with the surveyor, after you receive the official report, give them a call or visit them. Face to face, you can obtain considerably more information than that which appeared in the official document, and they will respond to your specific questions.

It is now time for you to make use of the surveyor's report in order to decide if this is the property for you and, indeed, to try to establish the price you will offer. If the surveyor has made it clear that there is a specific problem which will take a certain amount of money to put right, this will become a bargaining tool.

Bank manager

Selection of the bank you will use for borrowing and for future banking is a crucial decision. You may wish to start with your existing bank, since they know something of your banking trends and they have a profile of you. Getting to the business manager, however, may be more difficult. In my experience, they are not based in the local bank but can only be contacted by telephone. This is a major frustration for me, but it seems, this is a modern banking method embraced by most of the major banks.

In dealing with the bank, once again it is good to strike up a rapport with the business manager you are dealing with. Before meeting them, however, anticipate what they are likely to ask you. They will be interested in the following issues which in reality, will form the key ingredients of your business plan:

- Why do you want to go into business?
- What business are you considering?
- Do you have experience in this business?
- Have you identified the property you want?
- Has it been surveyed?
- Who will be the owners?
- What makes you think that customers will use your property rather than others?
- Have you analysed the competition?
- How will you make contact with potential customers?
- Have you prepared anticipated accounts for the first two or three years?
- What percentage of the purchase price do you have available and unencumbered?
- How much do you wish to borrow?
- Do you have any additional security on which to base a loan?
- What do you anticipate the payback period will be?

You can see that the answers to these questions are important to a lender and, and having gone through the business planning process, you are likely to have the answers.

The interview with the bank manager should not be a one-way dialogue. While they are interviewing you, you also are interviewing them to establish what products are available and what incentives there are for banking with this particular bank. As an example, when we started our business, we had no bank charges for the first year as an incentive. In the following year, we found that this was quite a saving since charges are made for banking every cheque, writing a cheque, direct debits, cash lodged (per £100), non-automated pay-ins and automated credits. It mounts up very quickly, so use this information as comparative data if you intend to talk to more than one bank.

Accountant

It may be logical to continue with the previous owner's accountant since they know the business and the property and will in fact be able to guide you in many ways. On the other hand, you may wish to make a break and deal with another accountant.

The role of the accountant is to prepare the accounts of your business in an acceptable format and to calculate the amount of tax you or the business must pay. In addition, they will advise on such things as dealing with the DSS, dealing with the Inland Revenue if you have employees, and recommending a bookkeeping system which is easy to operate and which gives the information in a format that makes their role less complex and therefore less expensive to you.

It is logical to deal with an accountant geographically close to you in order to maintain a fairly close relationship.

Insurance providers

It is likely that the bank will want to offer you a complete package which might include the insurance you require. However, it makes sense to obtain quotations for the insurance and to let the quoting companies know that they are one of a number of companies which will be asked.

You can obtain quotes yourself or can use a broker. You have a number of insurances and this can be time consuming, so time is saved by using a broker. List all the insurance needs you have and ask for a comprehensive quotation. In addition to vehicle insurance, property insurance is likely to cover such items as:

◆ property damage, including contents such as stock, personal contents, guest contents

- loss of revenue
- money (cash in house and in transit)
- employer's liability (essential if you have employees)
- public and products liability
- frozen foods
- loss of licence
- personal accident
- utilities failure.

Be sure to check that the personal contents of your own accommodation are covered. Generally, with a hotel policy they are not automatically covered although with a guest house or B&B, they normally will be.

Insurance is a very specialised field and the benefit of obtaining various quotes is that you can make a comparison and hopefully identify the areas which bear a high cost.

For most businesses, insurance cover is a cost you have to pay, which may never have any return. For others it is a huge benefit when a problem occurs. Remember, you only gain the upper hand on life insurance when you die!

Environmental Health Officers (EHO)

Over the years, I have had many contacts with EHOs and only when I realised that they were not the enemy, did I benefit from having a relationship with them. In Chapter 6, I will discuss this topic in more detail. However, at this point I would advise you to consider them as a part of your support team and work with them to make your premises safe.

When you are considering a property for purchase, ask the owner whether the kitchen has recently been inspected and whether any changes or repairs are pending and due to be carried out. If you are uncomfortable with the answer, contact the local EHO directly and ask them the question.

> Environmental Health Officers are part of your support team and should not be considered as the enemy but should be used to help you make your property safe.

Health and Safety Officers

In some jurisdictions, the EHO doubles and gives advice on health and safety issues. When we started our business, we received an extremely helpful folder from the Health and

Safety Executive which contained many leaflets about a range of issues relating to the health and safety of owners and employers. This was very comprehensive and covered issues such as alcohol problems, health promotion in the workplace, smoking policies for the workplace, food for a healthy workplace, promoting dental and oral health in the workplace, stress in the workplace and policy documents which related to these issues. Such information is very useful if you are employing staff and by applying them, the chances are that by creating a better working environment, you will keep your staff, to the benefit of your guests, you and your profits.

Licensing authority

If your property is licensed, then you or your spouse/partner will be required to become a licence holder. Your lawyer will make the application on your behalf. Generally, this is a formality, although in most cases, character references will be required. My local authority is, however, now requiring all licence applicants to undertake a training course and this relates to all, regardless of qualification and experience. Be sure to check the requirements of your local licensing authority through your lawyer.

If you need a licence where none currently exists, this is more complex. You will need planning permission, a building warrant and an environmental health certificate before the application can proceed. Your lawyer will advise on this process.

Inland Revenue

When I started my business, I was pleasantly surprised when I obtain an extremely comprehensive file called 'Starting Up In Business' from the Inland Revenue. This was particularly interesting to receive since I had been out of the country for many years and frankly, was not up-to-date with the UK tax situation. This is a very useable file, which is divided into four sections, namely:

◆ starting your business
◆ launching yourself into business
◆ growing your business
◆ maintaining your business.

Within each section, there is a great deal of information relating to good business practices as well as pointing out your obligation to pay tax, both personal or business tax and also VAT if your business is above that threshold. More on this in Chapter 9.

My accountant handles my tax affairs and prepares the returns. However, the information in this file will be of great benefit to you.

Fire safety

Your lawyer will check for you whether the property needs a fire certificate and indeed, if it does, whether one exists. Needless to say, this is important since if work needs to be done to comply with the fire department's requirements, then perhaps the purchase price should be adjusted. I recommend at an early stage in your possession of a hotel or guesthouse that you invite the local fire chief round to inspect the premises and let you know what can be done to make the property as safe as possible for the guests and you and your family.

Know how to use the equipment you have. Test your alarm on a weekly basis and let your guests hear it from time to time so they know what it sounds like. Rehearse an evacuation and know how to get guests out from each and every room.

Tourist Board and other quality advisors

No doubt, you will be a member of your local tourist authority and in order to obtain a certain level of recommendation, you will have to be inspected.

The 'quality assurance' concept is a good one and the more that can be done to obtain a generally high standard of accommodation, service and hospitality in your region, then the more likely that region is to attract new and returning guests.

Your first visit from a quality advisor will most probably be unknown to you in as much as they will make a reservation as a normal guest and will stay overnight. Only on checkout will they reveal that they are in fact a quality advisor from whatever organisation it is. This takes some of the nerve-racking aspect of the thought of an inspection away!

You can gain a great deal of information and ideas from your quality advisor who has the benefit over you in that they visit numerous properties every week and can therefore easily identify how your property fits in to the general level for the area. If you work positively with them, they will give you good advice on how to bring your standard up, although, if you listen to your guests, you may already have some quality assurance information.

Further details concerning the inspection process can be found in Chapter 4, which deals with quality issues, and in this section, you will learn how to gain from the quality assurance process.

Summary

I hope that this chapter has helped you to be analytical about your present situation and has enabled you to reach a conclusion about whether buying and running a small hotel or guesthouse is right for you. If you have already decided to proceed, then you have been presented with some ideas on how to minimise the risks of getting into business.

Most importantly, you have been introduced to the concept of the business plan. The exercise of preparing this document will take you through a very important thought process relating to your business idea. You cannot do it alone and you have been introduced to others who will assist you in getting it right and who can be classed as your 'support team'.

The following are the action steps for Chapter 1:

◆ Analyse your present circumstances.

◆ Analyse the advantages and disadvantages of having your own business.

◆ If necessary, gain relevant experience.

◆ Calculate how much unencumbered cash you have.

◆ Prepare a business plan.

◆ Investigate local competition.

◆ Prepare a short-term strategic plan from a SWOT analysis.

◆ Make your own description of what you want in the ideal hotel/guesthouse.

◆ Begin to select your support team.

CHAPTER TWO

Which Property and Which Business Format?

In Chapter 1, I suggested that you develop a profile of the kind of property you wish to purchase and the aim of this chapter is to assist you in doing exactly that. There are many options open to you and your decision is likely to be based on the funds you have available, the geographical location you wish to establish in and also, the technical skills you bring to the project. By that I mean whether you can carry out any necessary technical, construction work yourself.

Your age and fitness level might also be a factor as will your desire to operate in a city, with year-round business, or in a rural and possibly seasonal situation.

Hotel agents

When you are making a search, it is wise firstly to check the national hotel sales agents to see the range of properties and their locations that are available for sale. Some names are in the Appendix to this book. If you go into such a search with an open mind, it will help you to pinpoint the kind of property you wish to obtain and also the area. When you have decided on the area, also contact the local estate agents who will probably handle business as well as domestic properties.

If you already have a feeling for a particular area, you will be able to make a search within that area to find which existing properties are on the market. This can usually be carried out by area and price range. Do not be surprised if you see bigger properties for sale at a lower price than some small hotel/guesthouses. The reason for this is the year-round nature of larger hotels, as well as the need for staff, which mean it is more difficult to produce profit. The supply and demand aspect of smaller, easily managed businesses tends also to inflate the price although, in truth, it is generally easier to produce profit in such properties.

When you have spotted a business that appeals to you, contact the agent and ask for a fact sheet. This will give broad details of the business and will usually have outside and inside photographs as well as much more information. This information will usually include the following:

- **Asking price**. Usually phrased as 'offers over' or 'offers in the region of'.

- **Situation**. This will describe the location and may include a section of a map as well as road details showing the location of the business.

- **External areas**. This will describe what the property offers in terms of the grounds and will give some details of gardens and special features, as well as possibly some photographs.

- **The property**. This will describe in some detail the 'front of the house' including the bedrooms. It might give a feel for the décor and any unique aspects of the property.

- **Service area**. This will cover 'back of the house' information including kitchen, laundry, boiler room etc. Some details of equipment in these areas might also be given.

- **Owner's accommodation**. Details of the owner's private accommodation will be given with a description of the location in relation to the business end of the property.

- **Services**. This will describe the supply of utilities such as electricity, gas, oil and also the water supply and sewage arrangement.

- **Licence**. If licensed, the type of licence will be described.

- **Tenure**. This relates to the title, which is likely to be freehold or leasehold. Freehold would mean you own the property, while leasehold means the property is owned by someone else but you have rights to use it for the agreed period of time. Discuss these details with your lawyer.

- **The business**. This would describe the level of business that is achieved as well as give some information about where the business comes from. It might also give information about how the current holders operate and how many staff are employed.

◆ **Trading figures**. This generally gives the big picture, usually covering revenue, although possibly some agents' details will give a net profit with the notation that full accounts will be supplied to interested parties after viewing has taken place.

◆ **Additional information**. Some details may be given about how inventories will be handled after the sale takes place. It will give details of how the offer should be submitted. In addition, most agents have a link to companies or banks which are prepared to offer loans to facilitate the purchase.

> **Specialist hotel agents offer a very good service and they will assist you in finding the property you are looking for in the area of your choice. They make no charge to you since the charges for a sale are borne by the vendor.**

Buying a 'going concern'

There are many reasons why this is the most logical approach since it means that, from day one, you will be in business and taking in revenue. All the legal issues should be in place. Your lawyer should be instructed to check all of this for you. You should have approval from the Environmental Health Officer, from the fire service in the form of a fire certificate and if the property has a licence, then a transfer will be arranged at the next court sitting and you will be able to hold the licence, assuming the court sees you as a fit person. Some authorities are now requiring that licensees attend a training course, irrespective of previous experience.

You must not assume that work carried out in the past has been approved by the planning department so you must ask through your lawyer, as part of the purchasing process, for proof that all work has been authorised and is legal. If you fail to do this, and conversions are deemed to be unlawful, you are likely to be required to carry out additional work or to remove unlawful structures at a later date.

The design of the property has hopefully been planned so that operating as a business rather than a residence can be effective and efficient. You may see potential improvements for the future but you should be able to start up with the building as it is.

Create a business from home

You may already have a home which you feel can be developed into a business. However, this route is a complex one. Many issues exist relative to gaining permission from the planning authority of local government as well as other issues such as a fire certificate and environmental health permission. Zoning in a residential area may have restrictions, and it will be necessary to apply for a change of use.

In addition, you have to consider the conversion of what you have now into what would be acceptable to potential guests. They have requirements including en-suite rooms, safe parking, safety, heating or cooling when necessary, so all of these aspects must be taken into account.

Conversion will require the services of an architect who will liaise with the planning authorities on your behalf. This is not without cost, it should be pointed out. In some areas, local authority grants may exist and these are sometimes related to increasing employment within the area. The architect will probably be able to advise about such grants.

Location of the property

In the country

A business which is in a rural location will not appeal to guests who wish to be in a town, possibly within walking distance of shops, bars and restaurants. By the same token, however, some guests will select a country location because they want peace and tranquillity, and do not wish to be close to pubs, restaurants, shops and the general clamour of their fellow tourists. Such guests are likely to be longer-staying guests and will normally require dinner.

They will start by enjoying a good breakfast, followed by a busy day of walking or visiting the local attractions, returning 'home' to a nice pot of tea, followed by a bath or shower. After relaxing they will have worked up an appetite for dinner, perhaps preceded by a drink.

For you, there are some issues which relate to operating such a property, including proximity to suppliers, accessibility and closeness to both main roads, and, as far as the guests are concerned, to attractions which they might want to visit. There needs to be a compelling reason for them to want to stay in this particular property.

The proximity or otherwise of suppliers also brings up the issue of storage space for the commodities you need to operate your business. This will include planning accordingly for the right size of dry goods stores, refrigerator and freezer space. Look at the property with different eyes when looking at a more remote property, and try to establish how the remoteness affects the operation of the business. Prepare your questions for the vendors and get a feel for how similar they are to you, and whether what they enjoyed about the situation, is what would appeal to you. Consider also your social life and how the remoteness will affect this. If you are used to being able to drop in to the neighbours for a chat, consider that the nearest neighbours might be 20 kilometres away or on the other side of the loch! You may also have a harder sell to convince a lender that you can make a go of a business in a remote location.

The chances are that a country area is most likely to have seasonal trade, and this probably means you will have a number of months without business, unless some outstanding local attraction, such as Stonehenge, brings people to your area throughout the year. You might also consider creating off-season events and special interest attractions to generate some business in the off-season, as suggested in Chapter 8.

A benefit of a seasonal business is that after a busy season, probably with no days off and 14-hour days, there is time to rest and relax and then gradually become involved with the necessary maintenance activities, which can be carried out at a gentler pace. This also is the time for holidays and some quiet reflection on anything that went wrong last season and what can be done in the future to make sure that it does not occur again. At this time also the advertising plan for the next year should be put into action. Quite a lead time may be required for this.

The downside, of course, is that you have no money coming in and, if you have loans or a mortgage, this becomes quite a consideration. Your accountant, however, should have encouraged you to plan for higher payments during high season and lower payments for the low season, thereby compensating for the lack of business and income at this time.

In the country, staffing may be more difficult and, if you intend to work with some staff other than yourselves, look into the availability of potential staff members locally. The good aspect of this is that if you do get locals, they are convenient for you and the job you offer them is also convenient for them. Because of this they will generally do a good job for the benefit of the local position you offer.

In the city

A small hotel or guesthouse in a city is likely to be a year-round operation. In addition, there is a fair chance that the average stay will be shorter than in a country situation. This has three key outcomes that come to mind.

- Many room changes.
- Excess wear and tear, e.g. through more washing of bed linen, towels, etc.
- Less opportunity to get to know the guests and therefore create a bond, which usually leads to repeats and referrals.

Rates and the general cost of services will probably be higher in the city. The purchase price might also be higher in the city than the country, therefore the cost of servicing a loan will be higher. On the other hand, the price you charge for rooms and services may be higher, unless of course the number of available guesthouses or small hotels in the area forces the price down.

Condition of property

Pristine condition

If, like me, you do not have a technical bone in your body, then the attraction of purchasing a property in pristine condition is considerable. This will probably mean the purchase price will be higher, but the cost of maintenance and/or renovations over the next few years is likely to be reduced. This is not to say that preventive maintenance does not need to be carried out, but this will be discussed in Chapter 10.

From day one you can start operating without thinking about construction work, which is likely to overrun in time and cost. You can concentrate on developing routines and becoming efficient, as well as getting to know your guests and staff.

Needs renovation

The converse of the above is that, for the DIY fanatic or someone with building/technical skills, the purchase price is likely to be considerably lower for a property which is in need of renovations and there is scope to make changes to suit your ideas and needs.

It must be remembered that any major renovations you carry out are likely to require planning approval, and it is wise to work with an architect when considering this route following the purchase of the property. Prior to purchase, it is important to find out, through your solicitor, whether there are any restrictions on what work can be carried out on the property. The building may be listed, which may limit the changes you can make.

> **A few years ago, we looked into the purchase of a property which was a listed building and which had one room which had a different classification of listing, meaning that it could not be changed in any way. Look out for that kind of restriction.**

Upstairs and downstairs?

When my wife and I were looking for a property, prior to the one we now own, we omitted from our list of wants and don't wants, the issue of having stairs. We visited a property which we both liked very much that was on three levels. We had it surveyed and it came back with some dampness problems which put us off. Subsequently, we visited a property which was a bungalow, and only then did we realise the benefit of such a property. That was the one we purchased.

Apart from the obvious wear and tear on knees, there are some additional issues you may wish to consider relating to a property with several floors:

- storage space for the housekeeping materials on each floor or the purchase of a housekeeping trolley which can climb stairs
- possible need of a vacuum on each floor
- staff reaction to going up and down stairs
- guest reaction to going up and down stairs.

Another most important aspect of having a bungalow, as we subsequently found out, is that many guests have mobility problems and they are seeking a property with few, if any, stairs. This has, in fact, become a unique selling point for us and we use it in all the advertising we do, with positive results. I really believe that because of this we have longer stays from guests who are happy to have found a property which suits their limited mobility. It should be pointed out that not only elderly people have mobility problems. It has certainly brought us repeats and referrals, and that is the lifeblood of our business/ industry as I mention in Chapter 8.

Previous traditions

When purchasing a property, it is important to be able to continue the traditions of that property without too many radical changes which might upset the existing clientele. This, of course, does not need a great deal of consideration if the business was previously in a bad way, with little likelihood of referred and repeat business.

My advice here then is to make changes in a gradual way and not to reduce any services to which the existing clientele might take exception. As you progress in putting your stamp on the property, take a 'value added' approach and try to augment what already exists with your ideas and thereby offer an enhanced service.

One question which springs to mind is the possibility of taking over a guesthouse which has until now offered dinners when you have decided that dinners will no longer be offered. This clearly would have some negative effects and would be seen by existing customers as a reduced service. If you do not wish to offer dinners, consider a property which previously did not offer dinners.

Large grounds and gardens – or not!

Some friends of ours have a beautiful stone-built guesthouse with large grounds and gardens which take a lot of time and care to keep tidy. They operate strictly as a bed and breakfast and do not offer dinner other than on the odd occasion when guests stay about two weeks. They then occasionally invite the guests to join them for dinner without charge.

The interesting difference here between this operator and us is that in his previous life, he was a mechanical engineer and is very technically proficient, particularly with machines. In order to keep the grounds and gardens in top shape, he has a lot of equipment which he maintains and operates himself. The time he gains from not having dinners to prepare and serve, he spends in the garden. Some more thoughts on gardening are offered in Chapter 10. The loss of revenue from not having dinner sales and the sales of wines and drinks with dinner, he recoups through operating year round rather than seasonally as we do.

From this comparison, you can see that the choice of property has repercussions for the services you offer and the lifestyle you have following the purchase. Having said that, my friend has a greater growth opportunity if he decides to take on some staff and offer dinners and drinks. I suppose we also have some limited growth opportunity if we stayed open for a longer period.

The 'manor house' style of property

The idea of having a manor house as a small hotel or a guesthouse is very appealing and certainly has a draw for guests who want a real change of lifestyle for the period of their holiday. Generally, they are prepared to pay that little bit extra, although there is a chance that the price you have to charge reduces the size of the market niche.

We recently heard of a small hotel near us which had carried out some renovations in the off-season and then proceeded to double their room rates for the following season. This almost certainly changed the market niche but, by the same token, they now need half the previous amount of guests in order to achieve the same level of sales.

The 'manor house' type of business however may have some drawbacks. The reason why it is likely to be necessary to charge more is because of the added costs of running such a property. The style of the property lends itself to larger and older, possibly antique furniture. The rooms are larger and the cost of carpeting, soft furnishings, etc. and even cleaning might be higher, and there is likely to be a higher cost of heating, painting and general maintenance. Older properties have higher maintenance costs too, and there may be problems obtaining matching items for repairs, e.g. slates for the roof. Grounds might well be larger, raising the issues discussed in an earlier section of this chapter. Think how many 'tatty' old buildings you have visited that are screaming out for tender, loving care, which does not come without real investment. Generally speaking, an old property will need more care to keep it functioning, and there is also a greater likelihood of the need for staff.

The tenancy

Another option for someone with limited capital who is interested in a small hotel, is to consider the tenancy route. Brewery companies that own the small hotel/pub but see it mainly as an outlet for their beer and spirits sometimes offer tenancies. Their interest is not in running the business: they only want to sell their products.

For the tenant, this means that they will pay a rent for the property and also an 'ingoing', which is a price for the furniture, fittings and perhaps goodwill. This payment will probably be to the outgoing tenant. In the same way, if you take a tenancy, when you decide to leave, then you sell to the next tenant.

The restrictions, which apply to a tenancy, relate to having to buy the products of the 'landlord' company. This is part of the contract into which you enter. If the beer is not a popular one then this could be a problem, although often the local clientele get used to what is being served in their local bar.

Clearly, the key part of this business will be the sale of liquor so it should be understood that a tenancy is really a bar operation.

On the positive side, entry to the industry through this route is one of the least expensive methods, while the negative aspect is that no matter how much you do to build the business, any appreciation of the property value, due to your hard work, is not yours.

Other decisions

Another decision you will have to make which affects the type of property you take on, will be whether you want to accept animals. Usually this will relate to accepting dogs and, clearly, if you have no garden, then this becomes a problem. In addition, you must consider the cleaning implications following the stay and how this will affect the workload. On the other hand, if you have a property with good grounds for walking a dog, then this might be a feature you may consider as a marketing point. It might give you a unique selling proposition since so many properties now do not accept animals.

Another decision you might have to take is whether or not you will accept young children. Some properties are well suited to this and others are not. Family rooms in the house will suggest that children are welcome, but the lack of such facilities might suggest that this is a problem. A property which caters for families with children, will have to have safe play areas, possibly with swings and chutes, away from traffic. This should be considered during the property search.

The market niche of your business might be the key to making this decision. If you deal with an older clientele, it may be that they are looking for peace and tranquillity, and three or four children racing round the dining room might be at odds with this.

Legal considerations

The following legal requirements must be borne in mind:

◆ **Fire regulations**. More information is given in Chapter 10 about fire regulations. However, when you are looking at properties, have this issue in the forefront of your mind and most certainly, if you go to survey, be sure that all legal requirements are met. If the building is over three floors, look to see if there is a fire escape. Ask the vendor questions about the issue and ask to see the fire certificate. When you see a fire extinguisher, check that it has been inspected within the last year.

◆ **Change of use**. If you are considering making your home into a business, then clearly you need to have planning permission for any changes to be made, but in addition, you will have to obtain permission for change of use from a residential property to a business one. A simple check of the deeds of your house by a lawyer should tell you if the property can only be used as a residence.

◆ **Food hygiene regulations**. You will find more information in Chapter 6 about food hygiene issues. However, it should be pointed out that your local authority will inspect from time to time through the Environmental Health Officer. If you are inexperienced in this industry, you should attend a food hygiene course and obtain the necessary certificate as specified by your local authority. Remember that the last thing you want is an outbreak of a potential food-borne illness in your property.

Business formats

There are a number of ways that you can set up your small business and they have differences in terms of the methods of borrowing, methods of recording information, and indeed in terms of the financial risk.

Sole trader

When you have your property and you sign for it on the dotted line, assuming the property is ready to take customers, you can open the door and start doing business using your own name. If you register for VAT there are registration requirements, however if you intend to stay below the VAT level there are strictly speaking no rules about the records you keep. More about value added tax in Chapter 9. This is not to say you do not keep records, and in Chapter 9, I will suggest some records which you should keep. In addition, I recommend that you enrol the services of an accountant who will give you fuller advice on what records to keep.

The sole trader has the right to all profits but also is personally liable for all debts.

Partnership

A partnership exists when two or more people decide to start a business with the intention of sharing the profits. Setting up a business with another one or more persons can be done with few restrictions. A partnership is to all intents and purposes similar to a sole trader in that all partners are personally liable for debts even if the debts have occurred due to mismanagement by one of the partners. In the case of death of a partner, liability still exists, in this case through the estate of the deceased partner.

Clearly, before going into partnership, it is important to know the person or persons well and to have trust in them.

It might be wise for you and your partner to draw up an operational contract with a lawyer which might cover such issues as profit sharing, responsibilities and partnership cancellation period, i.e. period of notice. In addition, it may be wise to cover, in case it becomes necessary, how a partner can be removed from the partnership or how a new partner can be admitted.

Another difficult area, which needs some forethought, is the issue of a partner having a prolonged illness and how this might affect their share of profits. Holiday periods should also be considered.

It is conceivable that a partner may wish to withdraw capital from the business and this possibility should be discussed and written into a contract. Another issue might arise if a partner wishes to remove themself from the partnership and sell the share. First option to existing partners is common in this case.

As can be seen, a partnership which goes beyond husband and wife can be fraught with difficulties and it is recommended that a lawyer, who has experience of partnership and partnership difficulties is consulted, so that the contract is likely to cover all eventualities.

Limited company

The difference between the sole trader/partnership arrangement and the limited company is that the company is an entity in its own right, recognised in law. A key difference is that in the case of the business being unsuccessful and closing, the liability of the company is limited to the value of the assets of the company. The shareholders are not personally liable as individuals for the debts of the business. A company can be formed through a solicitor or even an accountant, or a dormant company can be bought, requiring possibly a change of name but also the naming of the new directors and establishing of the new articles of association.

Another key difference is that the company accounts must be audited and the company is liable to tax. The owners of the company effectively take a salary and they are liable to pay personal tax on this.

Summary

The aim of this chapter has been to help you decide on the ideal property for you and also to give some pointers on the business format which you may wish to use. There are numerous possibilities in purchasing a small hotel or guesthouse, and you must decide which suits your desired lifestyle, your experience and the location and environment you wish to live in. The business format should be discussed with your accountant to make the best decision.

The following are the action steps for Chapter 2:

◆ Compare and contrast the pros and cons of each property type in relation to your requirements for a property.

◆ Consider the legal conditions required for the property you have identified.

◆ Plan to consult with specialists such as surveyors, architects, lawyers and accountants for relevant advice.

◆ Make a decision on business format, in consultation with your accountant.

CHAPTER THREE

Getting Started

Pre-purchase experience

In the preface to this book and in Chapter 1, I recommended that you gain experience in the areas you consider to be your weakest. Remember that by spending some time working for someone else you are making mistakes at their expense, not yours, and you are learning from them. During this time, make notes on systems that you think work and those which do not. Take examples of any paperwork that you feel is useful and make copious notes about the good and the bad of what you have seen. All of this will help you more clearly define the systems and processes for your own property and create a paper trail similar to the one you have seen, if you feel it works well.

Take note of the routines that the operators have and try to analyse them and identify good practices and processes and those that are not so good. Begin to say to yourself, 'If that was up to me, how would I do it?' Sit down and then justify your reasons to yourself.

> Remember that from day one of your operation, you need to set up your routines and work methods, which will get the job done, hopefully in a way which will also give some free time for rest and relaxation.

Marketing and advertising issues before or on takeover

When someone is selling a business they have to face the fact that the property may not sell in the time frame they hope it will. This generally means that, because they might still be in the property the following year, they have to continue the pre-booking of the advertising space in the tourist authority guides and whatever else they normally advertise in. It is vital for you to check that this has been done as early as possible when you are making enquiries, since there are deadlines for getting into many of the publications.

In our case, we checked that the advertising was all in place and the vendor's lawyer communicated with our lawyer that the vendor would expect compensation for this pre-booked advertising at time of completion. This of course is negotiable, but our feeling was that it was an expense that related to our period of operation and we agreed that it was a legitimate expense, and so we paid for it at the time of purchase.

> **Failure to check that the advertising is in place in good time could well cause you a disastrous first year.**

Planning changeovers

When we took over our guesthouse, we arrived from abroad on Friday and the takeover date was the Tuesday. We stayed nearby before the takeover day.

The vendor had been extremely helpful and had informed all the relevant utility companies of the change of ownership and, in most cases, had received a response to confirm that they had the new details. We thought that would make life easy for us. WRONG! The transfer of the utilities went fairly well, but our major problem was the fact that we did not have a previous UK address. We were, therefore, unknown entities in the UK and so effectively had no credit rating. This made our life quite difficult. The biggest problem was the transfer of the telephone and, indeed, we were cut off for two days while I had to get letters from my lawyer to prove that I existed, as well as copies of my passport, etc. I offered to lodge cash in advance, but to no avail. The system was not geared for innovation.

Try to anticipate problems like this and make contact as early as possible in order to rule out any takeover day problems.

Let us look at the key potential problem areas and areas where continuity is vital:

◆ **Insurance**. In Chapter 1 I talked about the kind of cover you need. You can do your homework yourself or consult a broker but be sure you are clear about what you want and, most importantly, liaise with the vendor and ensure that the coverage is continuous with no break between owners. Remember Murphy's Law! Most companies will enable you to pay the premium by direct debit and this we find to be a benefit as well as spreading the cost over the year.

◆ **Electricity**. Contact the provider well in advance. Find out what they need from you. If you are from the UK they will probably only want to see a copy of your latest bill and then they know you exist. They can check your record of payments, and then they are able to open an account in your name without interruption of service.

◆ **Gas**. This would be similar to electricity.

◆ **Telephone**. This should be a similar process but take nothing for granted and communicate well in advance to ensure a transition without loss of service.

◆ **Email address**. Since all advertising and stationery, e.g. your letterhead etc. is likely to have the existing email address on it, you do not want to change it. This means discussions with the vendor and agreement that it can continue to be used. If it is their name then this needs to be changed at the earliest opportunity. A suitable label may be used to cover the email address on letterheads, brochures, etc. if large stocks remain. After obtaining agreement to use the email address, the next step is to contact the provider and have the address and password changed and transferred to you. This we found to be quite complex and at £1.00 a minute for support calls, it was quite expensive, but eventually was achieved. At this time, it might be a good idea to arrange a link to an account which you can use worldwide in order to pick up business emails, even when you are away from the property, e.g. on holiday in Bermuda!

◆ **Website changes**. If you are taking over a website, you will want to make obvious changes immediately such as the owner's names and any changes to the operation and/or prices that you are putting into effect. At a later date, you may wish to sit with your webmaster and make more radical changes. However, initially these simple changes should be made just to remain current.

◆ **Local tourist board**. As early as possible, make an appointment to meet with your local tourist board personnel and, again, check that all the information they hold is current and applicable to the operation as you intend to run it. If you feel you have time to become involved in their committees, mention this at the time, but my advice would be to hold back on this until you are clear in your mind about the time you might have available.

- **Rates**. Liaise with the local authority regarding rates, so that they arrange for the changeover of ownership in their records, thus ensuring that at a later date they do not produce a large bill which you should have been paying monthly or quarterly. This also can be paid by direct debit mandate and this means you can more or less forget it, therefore gaining the cash flow benefit of not paying it all up front.

- **Satellite television**. If the transfer of the system has been part of the sale, then the company should be notified of your name for their bills. Remember that this will be necessary for your accounting purposes. Be aware that the television company will want payment for 'sale' of their product, if it is available in guest rooms.

- **TV licence**. Check to see that you have a 'hotel' licence. For up to 15 rooms it is the same price as a domestic one.

- **Suppliers**. While it is not vital to inform them immediately, it is good business practice and common courtesy to contact all suppliers to give them details of the names of the new owner so that from day one, all invoices are correctly addressed for the benefit of the accounting process. You may wish to change suppliers but inform the present suppliers anyway.

- **Keys**. It is vital to inspect the keys for all areas of the property and make sure they are appropriately tagged. This takes time and it is important to allow the time to do it. Try every key in the locks to be sure that everything is as it says it is. Remember, when the vendor jumps into their car, you cannot ask any more questions easily. Enquire if they are aware of any missing keys. Find out if there is a neighbour who is a 'key-holder' and whether they are happy with the fact that this person is the key-holder. Also ask if there is anything they would change in their control of keys. If you have any doubts after you have gone over these issues, make a decision about whether you feel it would be wise to change at least the outside locks. While this would be an added cost, it might also give you peace of mind. Arrange to meet the key-holder as soon as possible.

- **Safe**. If a safe is part of the inventory, find out how the combination is changed and change it.

- **Staff**. If you are 'taking over' any staff, it is important that you have asked the vendors about their abilities and, if possible, it is wise to interview them in advance of the takeover. This will dispel any apprehension they may have and give you an opportunity to get over your ideas on the future of the business.

◆ **Contacts**. Ask the vendor to give you a list of suppliers and tradesmen that they would recommend and their contact numbers. You may want them to attach to them a 1 to 5 rating just so that you know who to work with and who to consider replacing.

◆ **Cash and carry**. Open an account at the cash and carry.

◆ **Paper and marketing supplies**. Check how soon brochures will be needed as well as things like letterhead, registration forms, guest bills, etc. If urgent, arrange for an order in your name to be delivered on or just after the takeover date. Remember that the vendor will have reduced costs by running down supplies as much as possible.

There are a number of other agencies, which need to be notified that you are now in business:

◆ You must register with the Inland Revenue's Contributions Agency in order to switch to self-employed National Insurance contributions.

◆ If relevant to your business, you must register with the Custom and Excise's VAT office.

◆ You must inform the local environmental health office that you have taken over the business or that you are starting a business. If it is a new business, you will, ideally, have been working closely with them as the building or renovations have been taking place.

◆ You must register with the Inland Revenue and your accountant will no doubt do this on your behalf.

◆ You must inform the local authority in order to be assessed for Council Tax.

Opening bank account(s)

You may already have an account at a local bank, in which case you know the local staff and possibly you have been in touch with them regarding a loan or an overdraft. It is logical therefore that your account for the business should be opened at this branch.

Regardless of any loyalty you might have to any particular bank as a retail customer, it makes good sense to shop around the banks to see who will offer you the best arrangement for your business and for your business account.

For the business, you will want a current account and, depending on rates of interest in various accounts, you may wish to have an investment account for the business, which may gain better interest for any cash retained in the account. As your current account grows, make regular transfers to the higher interest investment account. Depending on your outgoings and particularly on loan interest and capital repayment levels, you may have a considerable opportunity to gain interest, particularly during your high season.

When you open the current account you will receive a chequebook and a debit card. I recommend you also arrange for a credit card for each partner for the benefit of slowing the payment process and therefore improving cash flow. You will save charges by having the entire outstanding amount paid by direct debit from the account on a pre-selected due date every month. An additional benefit of using a credit card is the reduction of charges to your account every time a cheque or a debit card transaction is made. On the credit card for the month, you may have thirty entries, but the single direct debit payment in the bank account, reduces the charges.

Inventories

The inventory of furniture and fittings should have been provided before you made an offer for the property. It is important that you study this carefully so that you are indeed purchasing what you think you are purchasing. Frequently, an information sheet for a business will say something like 'an inventory will be provided of all personal items which are not included in the sale'. This should be checked so that you are sure you know what you are going to receive. There may be a painting that you felt gave character to the lounge or a piece of antique furniture in the hallway that fitted beautifully. If you have not been careful, you will be disappointed when you find these articles are not there on takeover day. Remember that if you are taking over a going concern that means that you should be able to walk in and start trading.

In the takeover of a small property, inventory or stock in hand to be transferred from the vendor to the purchaser, may not be a big issue. This tends to be more of an issue where a bar is concerned, although it is general practice for the vendor to run down the stock of all items in hand. We are talking about consumables here rather than equipment and items, which would be classed as assets. Sometimes, an advertisement for a property will state a price for the purchase and SAV meaning stock at valuation on the date of the transfer of the business. Consumables will include foods, beverages including alcoholic, and cleaning materials. The expectation is that the purchaser will pay the vendor for these items, which the vendor has bought but which will be used by the purchaser.

In a big takeover, an independent stock-taker will sometimes be hired to value the stock. For a small property, it is unlikely that this will be necessary. If you, the purchasers, are taking over in the closed season in the case of a seasonal hotel, you can ask the vendor not to leave any stock, so it is not an issue. On the other hand, if the takeover is during a period when the property is up and running, you may request that they leave the normal ongoing stock. This may be particularly important where there is a considerable lead-time in obtaining items, e.g. if it is a rural property where there are limited deliveries.

For a smaller property, it is likely that the vendor will have listed all stock items to be transferred, will have checked the invoice prices paid for these items and by multiplying the quantity with the unit price, will have achieved the value.

As far as you, the purchasers are concerned, you should check that:

◆ The stock as stated is what is there for transfer.
◆ The prices are correctly stated.
◆ The items are in good condition and not past sell by date.

It becomes quite important to do this thoroughly, and you should allow time for doing this. Be prepared to be picky and eliminate items that you feel are old and cannot be used. It is a sad reflection on human nature, but sometimes, someone will try to pull a fast one on you, particularly if they feel you bargained well against them on the purchase price of the property.

Finally, since the stock will have been run down, make sure you know what wines etc. are available for day one, and consider making an order to arrive on day one in your name. Try to avoid being out of everything that a guest might order, both for their sake and for your confidence.

Pre-bookings/deposits

As an ongoing concern, the business will have a reservations system, which must be passed over to the incoming proprietor. You will have seen this before, in order to gauge the level of business. Now, it becomes one of the most important tools in your operation. Again, time is required to sit down with the vendor and equate the reservations in the system with relevant correspondence in the file. It is useful for you to find out as much as you can about the guests who are in the system.

> You will want to know who the regular repeat guests are. Do they have any particular requests that you should know about? Are there any special diets to be catered for?

Most important at this stage is to establish the deposits that have been paid in advance and be sure that this is recorded in the reservation system, so that when the guest checks out, the correct deposit is deducted from the bill. Any deposits paid are in fact your property and the vendor should pay you for them, or the lawyers should make the relevant credit for deposits in the final calculation at the completion point.

Takeover day

Butterflies in the stomach are part of the norm for this day. I would say that if you do not have them, something is wrong. They are probably the result of a sleepless night and doubts about whether you have thought of everything, as well as whether you are doing the right thing. The good news is that you are going to be so busy getting to know your business and your property that they will soon be gone.

You will have prepared a checklist of items that have to be done and you will have prearranged a number of things.

'To do' today will include:

♦ Checking the stock as described above. Agreeing and paying for stock.

♦ Checking furniture and fittings inventory against original inventory.

- Checking furniture and fittings inventory of bedrooms, bathrooms, kitchen, public areas etc.

- Checking equipment for idiosyncrasies.

- Thoroughly checking the keys and identifying any potential problems.

- Agreeing the cost of advance advertising.

- Ascertaining if any contacts need to be made urgently.

- Agreeing and checking deposits received.

- Learning how to work things like the boiler, the safe, etc. Remember Murphy's Law!

- Obtaining a list of contacts and numbers of 'recommended' suppliers and tradesmen.

- Meeting with the staff.

- Asking 'Is there anything else I should know?'

- The formal handover, presumably in the presence of the vendor with their and your lawyer.

After the vendor has gone and the champagne has been consumed, perhaps you have dinners to prepare and serve, or perhaps you arranged to take over at an off-season time or purposely arranged not to have any guests. These possibilities are worth considering. If you have guests to serve, get to work and prepare meals that you are comfortable with. Set the tables and be familiar with the location of anything you might need. Scan the beverage and wine list to avoid looking silly when you are asked to recommend a wine with the duck!

After dinner service, set up the dining room for breakfast and prepare your 'breakfast box' in the fridge for the morning with all the necessary items, some of which may have to be taken from the freezer.

Walk the property and check that windows and doors are locked.

Set the alarm for 07.00a.m. and have a good night's sleep!

Day One of the operation

The first day's routine will depend on the level of business, if any, but if you have guests, deal with them through service and checkout as required. Establish whether any guests will be having dinner. Check the paperwork for incoming guests to see if any dinners have been requested, and plan for dinners if required.

- Carry out the housekeeping duties and begin to formulate a schedule for each person based on their 'areas of operation' (see the next section to visualise a schedule).

- Contact suppliers to inform them of the takeover if this was not done by the vendor. A standard letter may well suffice in this instance.

- Check stocks and make orders for anything that is needed, or visit the cash and carry.

- Spend time with guests as appropriate.

- Take time for meals. Beware the dangers of missing meals and, whatever happens over the next few days and weeks, be sure to eat well and take the time to relax and talk about the activities of the day at a meal. Your calorie usage will almost certainly increase and the chances are you will lose weight if your previous job was more sedentary.

- At the end of the day, have a debriefing session together to iron out any issues that need to be resolved.

Creating a routine

Clearly the events of the day force a routine on you. However, you must begin to manage your time in order to find a little bit for rest and relaxation. The following is the one we use and while this must remain flexible, every day is based around this routine. Needless to say, things will, from time to time, cause a problem which means that the routine goes out of the window. Solve the problem and get back to the routine as soon as possible. A problem-solving process is shown in Chapter 9 and it works in every problematic situation.

There are some specific things which we believe it is important to do in order to lighten the load and to keep communication intact. We make beds together since this is considerably easier with two people than with one, and this means that we have the opportunity during the housekeeping time to talk about things that are going on.

There is a danger that if your paths do not cross, one might be wondering what the other is doing and thinking that all the work seems to be going one way. In order to prevent this becoming an issue, work together as much as possible.

If things are relatively quiet and the house is fully booked up with no expected arrivals, take the opportunity to go for lunch if you can possibly find the time. Take a break and get away from the property yourself. Have an answering machine and have any telephone calls recorded. It is simple to change the message and customise it in a friendly way and always return the call as soon as you return if any have been left. 'We are just escaping for an hour for lunch but please leave your name and number and we will get back to you very soon'!

The routine shown in Figure 3.1 below, then, seems very pedantic and detailed. However, I am using this to make the point that a routine is very important in order to be efficient, and to release some personal time for you and your spouse.

Clearly, if you have staff, then another routine has to be planned which, inevitably, should include more personal time coupled with some supervisory duties to ensure that the standard you want is being met. If not, as explained in Chapter 11, the likelihood is that some training time will need to come into the plan.

Another aspect of this chart is to make you think of where your skills are best suited so that the tasks that become part of the routine are ideally distributed.

Do what you are good at and what you enjoy, and share equally the less desirable tasks, which nonetheless need to be carried out.

The schedule may seem unrelated to you and your property but I feel that it is useful to begin to formulate either in your mind or on paper some kind of routine if for no other reason that to avoid the 'headless chicken' syndrome that often happens in our industry.

Unlike working in a bank, where you wait outside in the morning until someone unlocks the door and then have to leave in the evening so someone can lock up, this industry has endless hours available to you to be at work. If you do not have a routine, you will amble around dabbling at the tasks that have to be done and perhaps you will never

Partner A	Partner B
Morning 7.30 to 9.45	Morning: 7.30 to 9.45
Breakfast set-up in kitchen.	Breakfast buffet set-up in dining room.
Cooking of some items just before service.	Milks, butters, condiments on tables.
Receiving orders, preparing breakfast to order.	Greeting guests, taking orders, serving juices
Washing up, clearing and putting everything in	and cereals. Collecting cooked foods, teas,
its correct place.	coffees etc.
After last main dish is served, washing of pots	Loading dishwasher as dishes are returned to
and pans that remain. Clean kitchen.	kitchen.
Strip beds and start washing machines.	Offer menu and take dinner orders.
Find time to talk to guests.	Deal with bills and checkouts.
Say goodbye to guests.	Chat with departing guests.
	Strip beds and start washing machines as
	rooms are vacated.
Morning 10.00 to 13.00	Morning 10.00 to 13.00
Make up or change beds.	Put away breakfast items.
Dust and tidy guest rooms.	Change table clothes.
Clean showers, toilets and basins.	Reset dining room for dinner.
Change or fold towels.	Tidy and vacuum dining room, hallways and
Tidy and clean reception area.	reception area.
Hang out laundry.	Stock bar as required.
Prepare banking.	Restock hospitality trays for rooms.
Respond to request for brochures and confirm	Help with bed making.
reservations.	Vacuum bedrooms.
Have lunch (very important).	Have lunch (very important).
13.30. to 15.00	13.30. to 15.00
Iron bed linen.	Banking. Sometimes together.
Store bed linen.	Shopping. " "
Arrange flowers throughout.	Post office. " "
	Advanced preparation of food for dinner.

Figure 3.1. Plan for a day's routine.

Partner A	Partner B
15.00 to 18.00	**15.00 to 18.00**
Relaxing.	Relaxing.
Waiting for arrivals.	Waiting for arrivals.
Greeting and check-ins.	Greeting and check-ins.
Check garden — tidy planters, hanging baskets, etc.	Water plants and hanging baskets.
	Tidy outside areas.
18.00 to 19.00	**18.00 to 19.00**
Prepare to cook.	Prepare cold starters.
Casseroles earlier.	Open bar.
Prepare sauces in advance.	Fill ice bucket.
Start cooking process.	Respond to calls for pre-dinner drinks.
19.00 to 21.00	**19.00 to 21.00**
Prepare and serve food on request.	Offer wine list, take orders, serve wine and other drinks.
Prepare desserts.	Serve starters, main dishes, desserts.
Load dishwasher.	Make and serve coffee and tea.
Wash pots and kitchen implements.	Assist with kitchen cleaning.
Visit guests in dining room.	As tables clear, change cloths and reset for breakfast.
Prepare breakfast box.	
Wash floor and disinfect worktops.	
21.00 onwards	**21.00 onwards**
Attend to any necessary correspondence.	Serve drinks as required.
Write and print tomorrow's dinner menu.	Put out lights in dining room when clear.
	Mail any responses to enquiries.
	Check the property outside and in.
	Set corridor nightlights.

Figure 3.1. (contd.)

get them done. Meanwhile, the hours roll on!

Work on your joint routine and share the work equitably. Base it on skills so that each person is involved in things they enjoy doing.

Summary

Anticipate as much as possible in order to make the early days as straightforward as you can. Like a new job, taking over your own business will be a change in lifestyle and initially, a stressful and physically demanding one. Do what you can to eliminate problems, stress and exhaustion. Develop good working routines and try to stick to them for long enough to test them out. Keep an open mind, however, and be flexible. Make adjustments if necessary and try again. Do not miss meals and see them as a period of relaxation and communication.

The following are the action steps for Chapter 3:

◆ Prepare a checklist of important issues that need to be discussed with the vendor.

◆ Meet the vendor with the checklist and in discussion, become familiar with each of the issues.

◆ Allocate if possible some of the changeover issues to the vendor (with their cooperation). Contact suppliers etc.

◆ Obtain good information regarding reservations and deposits and agree the method of deposit transfer.

◆ Plan takeover day.

◆ Plan day one.

◆ Prepare to plan an operating, day-by-day routine.

CHAPTER FOUR

Setting Your Standard

Understanding the concept of 'quality'

'Beauty is in the eye of the beholder' is a phrase we all know and understand, yet if you ask a group of managers what they understand by excellence they will trundle out comments like 'the ultimate', 'highest quality', etc. and if you ask for examples, they will mention Rolls Royce, The Savoy, Mercedes and other elite brand names.

I mention this because you will be interested in offering your guests a quality stay. The question, however, that you must ask yourself is 'What are they looking for?' What are their needs, wants and expectations when they come to your guesthouse or small hotel? What is vital is that you, the operator, do not try to force upon them something that will not satisfy these needs, wants and expectations.

In my experience, when I was an advisor to the industry, I found many small businesses getting into trouble because a 'new to the industry owner' tried to impose his standard or what he thought was quality on his guests, and it simply was not what they wanted. The result was that they did not return and did not do the business any good in terms of positive referrals. Many of these businesses simply did not survive.

So what is a good definition of quality? **Delivery of the standard you feel is right for your guests, every time**. This is a simple, yet useful definition to consider using and what it means is that you identify what your customers want and deliver it consistently. You do not do what you want. You do what the customers want and you get it right the first time and every time thereafter. The standard is what you offer in your establishment because you have established that this is what your customers want. For example: When we took over our guest house, we found that breakfast was offered between 8.30 and 9.00a.m. We were uncomfortable with this. However, we tried it and found that we could not individually prepare the food to the standard we felt our guests would expect without pre-preparation and therefore lower quality. We also began to get requests for early breakfast and, on occasions, when guests checked in and we told them breakfast time, they made it clear with sighs and grimaces, that 9.00 would be difficult for them to make. We, therefore, made a decision to extend the breakfast period from 8.00 to 9.30a.m and we prepare breakfast to order, producing a high standard and we satisfy the desires of our guests.

The upside of this decision is satisfied guests while the downside is that it takes more of our time, but we are prepared to live with that.

What customers want

Finding out what customers want is a highly complex process for large manufacturing and service companies. They spend a lot of money in creating marketing departments which survey guests and hold focus groups to establish what their customers think of their product or service, so that they can plan for change in order to better satisfy the customer base.

In a guesthouse, you do something similar, but less formal. You talk to them and you listen to them! This is a less formal process than the hotel groups with marketing departments use but it is more effective since you are listening to your guests yourself, and you are the decision maker. The large groups have many levels of hierarchy between the customer and the ultimate decision-maker and hence, the message becomes garbled. The decision made may then be based on invalid information, with the result that little is done that benefits the customer.

Case study

I will take the time to emphasise this point by telling you about something that happened a number of years ago. I became involved with a hotel that had decided to upgrade its menu. The way this was done was for the general manager to meet with the executive chef and discuss the concept. From there, the chef met with his sous chef and a few of the other chefs. The chefs came up with a prototype menu. The availability of ingredients was checked and the dishes were tested and costings made. Next, the dishes were served to the general manager and some of his associates and comments and changes made in consultation with the chefs until the menu was finalised. The menu was printed and prepared and, a few days before the start of the new menu, a training session was held with the service staff to inform them of the ingredients of each dish and the service style.

I hope you have spotted the deliberate mistake! No input from the guests, however, since it can be quite difficult to obtain information from guests, we should use the next best thing, the food servers. They take the orders, they listen to the guests, and they see the expressions of disappointment or delight on their faces. They listen to their complaints, but seldom tell the kitchen staff for fear of the wrath of the chef. They listen to regular guests who tell them of their boredom with the menu and what they would like to see available instead.

Did the general manager and the executive chef consider talking to the waiters? Not on your life, yet there was the source of the information needed to make effective changes to the menu. When I became involved, we started the other way round by having meetings with the service staff as well as regular guests, and got them involved in, and enthusiastic about, the process of change. They helped to plan a very successful menu.

Hospitality issues

The concept of hospitality is one which is fairly easy to define and not always easy to deliver day after day, particularly if you are a two-man team. To some extent, it might mean that someone has to be in the property all the time since it could be considered inhospitable to make use of an answering machine. Decisions have to be made on how far you will go to be available to guests and potential guests. If you are not always going to be available to answer the telephone, then the message must be warm, friendly and efficient and must make some kind of promise that the call back will be as soon as possible, and you must make sure that it is.

Similarly, if a request is received for a brochure, it should be dealt with and sent the day it is requested. Not only is this courtesy, but it may put you ahead of the other properties the guest has contacted. It is good business practice.

The greeting of the guests on arrival is most important to make them feel welcome and introducing yourself, possibly in the car park is a nice touch. Try to have a system where you can spot the arrival and be there as they get out of the car. Our kitchen overlooks the car park and that is a plus as far as that goes.

You should make a decision about what you want to be called. If you introduce yourself by your first name then this brings an informality that the guests generally find to be comforting and homely. If they offer their first name, then use that also.

Help with the luggage. In some cases, the guest will want to see the room first, so take them in and show them the room. While there, set up the luggage stand in readiness for the cases coming. Offer to help with the cases and bring them in and place them in the room.

It is a nice touch to offer a pot of tea and biscuits or scones on arrival in the lounge. Guests probably need this after a long drive and it builds a relationship as you chat with them. This is a good time to tell them about the property, what is offered, what the region offers and where to obtain information. It is wise to have a checklist of information to be presented to guests, which becomes automatic. You can run through this informally during the time you are having a chat with them on arrival. Think of this process as being similar to the induction process of a new employee at work when they start a new job.

During this time, you can try to sell the idea of having dinner during the stay, assuming the guests had not previously booked for it. Always have available the menu and wine list as well as any special features you offer, such as, perhaps, your selection of special beers or single malt whiskies. If you offer packed lunches for walkers or any other similar service point it out at this time.

At mealtimes, greet guests positively and, if appropriate, and if it seems that the guests want some interaction between each other, introduce a general topic of conversation and let them pick up on it and chat to each other. My experience is that this works most of the time, bearing in mind that you are in and out of the dining room, going backwards and forwards to the kitchen during the evening. Such a situation can be good for beverage sales as guests will sit longer and have drinks as they talk.

As guests leave, help them to the car with luggage and have a pleasant chat with them before they go. This is all time consuming, but for the guests, the relationship they have built with you is part of their memory of their holiday.

Never forget that the business we are in is one of memories. There is little tangible evidence of a holiday, other than photographs and the odd souvenir. It is the memories that your guests retain that give value to their experience with you.

In short, hospitality towards guests relates to showing a genuine friendliness and even kindness, which makes the guests feel they are special. In larger properties, dealing with many staff, this is not always easy, but with a small operation, it can be achieved well with a bit of thought and a genuine desire to please.

I often tell youngsters going into the hospitality industry that in many other jobs and careers, the employee never hears a word of thanks from anyone and this can make the job soul destroying. In our industry, showing good hospitality means the chances are you get grateful thanks on a daily basis from your guests and this is truly good for the ego!

One final note on this subject is to mention how to handle complaints. It is to be hoped that this will be a very unusual experience. However it is worth looking at a tried and tested approach to such a situation. This might well form the basis for training for any staff member.

Only too often, when a guest has a complaint, the receiver of the complaint immediately takes up an attitude and the barrier comes up, as is shown, for example, by the case of folding the arms. The best approach, however, is as follows:

- Listen with empathy. Make and hold eye contact.
- Show empathy. 'I understand', 'I'm so sorry', etc.
- Clearly identify the problem and repeat it to be sure you have it right.
- Decide what the guest wants and if it is feasible.
- Explain to the guest what you can do and obtain agreement.
- Learn from the complaint and if it is clearly a genuine problem, solve the problem so that it does not happen again.

While this will work in most cases of genuine complaint, it should be made clear that sadly, there are some people who have a policy of complaining in order to obtain some kind of tangible gain. You have to decide in each individual case what you will do for this person and how you will solve the situation.

Price/value relationship

In Chapters 1 and 8, I discuss pricing, but it is worth mentioning in this chapter about quality, that when guests pay the bill, they want to have the feeling that it has been good value. Some years ago, a change took place in our industry in that it became much more difficult to raise prices and indeed, what was happening was that prices remained static, and in order to compete, the concept of value added was introduced.

What this meant is that for the price, guests were offered extras as an inducement to stay at that particular property. This is now unlikely to go away and so to be competitive, on top of your unique selling proposition, you need to have value added inducements.

Such inducements might include a glass of wine with dinner or extra amenities in the bathroom such as shampoos, sewing kits, etc. It has gone further now in that many properties make such offers as a fourth night free. When the guests work out the calculation, chances are that if everything else was positive about the stay, they will feel that the price/value relationship was good.

Importance of systems and procedures

Since achieving quality means getting whatever you are doing right the first and every time thereafter, it is logical that you have in place, systems and procedures which will enable you, or anyone who takes over from you, to come up with the same result.

Performance standards help to achieve this and as time goes on, you should try to develop them. In the same way that you write a recipe which has ingredients and the method of preparation, you can produce a standard or recipe for cleaning a toilet, setting a table or opening a bottle of wine.

To begin with, this standard is perhaps in your head, but as you have time to do it, write it down. This becomes the basis for the training of staff if you decide to go down that route at some point. It will also help the standard stay the same if you and your spouse/partner decide to be multi-function operators and switch jobs at some point.

Standards develop and evolve as you obtain feedback from your guests and this evolution should be written into the standard in order to stay up to date.

Inspections and quality assurance

While the first visit from the quality assurance arm of your tourist authority or assessment agency can be nerve wracking, it ought not to be so, since their aim is the same as yours, in that they want you to be the best you can be. On the other hand, you might avoid this pressure if the quality advisor checks into your hotel incognito!

In Chapter 6, in the section on hygiene, I recommend that you see the value of the Environmental Health Officer's visit and learn from it in order to avoid any problem related to hygiene issues. In the same way, the quality advisor's main task is to help me to monitor or improve the quality and condition of my property so that the guests will be satisfied with their stay. I would go so far as to say that their reporting process helps to give structure to the various tasks involved in running the property and helps identify key areas where critical points exist relating to the level of guests' satisfaction.

A recent survey on restaurants indicated that the two top issues on which guests rate them are cleanliness and hospitality. It was interesting that the reason for going into the restaurant, the food, did not feature in the two top choices. This perhaps gives us a clue as to key issues for us in our guesthouse operation.

There are a number of definitions to be found regarding guesthouses and the following is the one from my grading authority: 'A guesthouse is usually a commercial business and will normally have a minimum of four letting bedrooms of which some will have en-suite or private facilities. Breakfast will be available and evening meals may be provided.' This is the definition that potential guests see when they look in their guide to accommodation for the local area. This tells them very briefly what to expect. The fact that the guesthouse is graded, however, means something else, and they can judge by the number of stars, diamonds, crowns, forks or whatever, the level of quality of the establishment. The higher the grading, the higher the expectation of the guest, but also the standard expected by the quality advisor.

Some assessment instruments respond to questions and some have headings which expect a comment. For example, in one of our assessments, a question is used under the heading cleanliness which asks 'Were toilets clean and fresh smelling?' while another simply has a heading 'Bathrooms' and the inspector makes comments and gives a grading on a numerical basis. In this instance, an overall grading for the property under all the headings is established.

The formulas are different. However, the aim is the same. It is not to give you a hard time and to make you feel bad. It is to investigate your property systematically and then sit down with you and give you help and guidance to reach your own quality goals. I have gained a great deal of information from the quality advisors we have seen, even about where to purchase items, as well as guidance on best quality for certain uses. Bear in mind that they visit many properties in the course of a week and they therefore have a very good comparative base to be able to help you conform or excel.

Our regional tourist authority, previously known as the Scottish Tourist Board and now known as VisitScotland has a fairly comprehensive quality assurance process under different categories of accommodation or business. For each area, they have guidance notes for operators, which enable the operators to match their property with the required standard. This helps the operator to prepare their strategic plan for improvement more effectively. Clearly you cannot do everything at once and, by simply having two lists, side by side, i.e. what exists now and what is the ideal, you can identify the gaps in what you offer and plan to rectify the situation through prioritisation of work and/or purchases.

Each of the regional tourist organisations helps their constituents with similar advice. However in the following section, I will highlight the criteria used for the guesthouse sector with VisitScotland. The considerably more detailed information can be found at the website www.scotexchange.net/BusinessDevelopment. After this, select

Quality Assurance Schemes. I recommend having a look at this site. The information that follows here is from this website, reproduced to help explain how a quality assurance scheme works for the benefit of the guest and the operator.

The following extract is from the above named website under the heading 'Guesthouse' although the first section describes more closely the B&B. operation. Yet another Introduction and General Criteria exists for the 'Small Hotel' category. Please be aware when reading any of this that criteria and details offered by agencies such as this are likely to change from time to time and it is important to keep abreast of the changes.

Introduction and general criteria

The VisitScotland criteria states the following:

> A guesthouse will normally have a minimum of four letting bedrooms, of which at least 20% will have en-suite or private bathroom facilities. Breakfast to be available and evening meals may be provided. It will normally have a fire certificate and be commercially rated.

Criteria for Classification

In addition it has a 'Criteria for Classification' which covers many different areas of importance, nine of which are indicated below. I am presenting the following in detail since this will help you in assessing any property which you may be considering for a business as well as helping you comply more easily when you take the next step of owning a business.

The nine sections, shown in Figure 4.1, then, give guidance to operators on what level they are achieving.

Quality advisor's visit

When the quality advisor visits a property, they consider eight separate areas to come up with the final grading report. One of the sections is 'Bedrooms' and within this section are the sub-sections:

♦ decoration
♦ furnishings and furniture
♦ flooring
♦ beds, linens, bedding

1. Safety and security
The entrance should be clearly identified, preferably with lighting above the doorway. There should be a high degree of general safety and security, including information on procedures in the event of an emergency.

In addition there must be printed details of how to summon assistance in the event of an emergency at night.

Adequate measures should be taken for the security of guests and their property. There should be a means of securing bedroom doors from the inside and out with a key available for entry. Guests must be able to exit the bedroom without the use of a key.

Adequate levels of lighting should be provided for safety and comfort in all public areas, including sufficient light on stairways and landings at night.

Particular attention should be given to the safety and security of guests occupying ground floor accommodation.

2. Cleanliness
A high standard of cleanliness should be maintained throughout the property. Particular attention should be given to bathrooms, shower rooms and toilets.

3. Maintenance
Buildings, their fixtures, furnishings, fittings and exterior and interior décor, must be maintained in a sound, clean condition and must be fit for the purpose intended.

All electrical equipment should be safely maintained and in good working order.

4. Annexes
Where an establishment has an annexe, the facilities provided in the annexe will be taken into account in the assessment of the establishment.

Paths or passageways to the annexe must be in good condition, well surfaced and adequately lit.

Visitors must be advised at the time of booking, or subsequently in the event of a change, if the accommodation offered is in an unconnected annexe, or has separate external access. The location of such accommodation should also be indicated.

5. Reservations and prices
There should be friendly and efficient service appropriate to the style of accommodation. All enquiries, requests, reservations, correspondence and complaints from visitors should be handled promptly and courteously.

It should be made clear to visitors exactly what is included in the prices quoted for accommodation, meals and refreshments, including service charge and other surcharges, e.g. credit cards.

A leaflet or brochure should be available.

The price agreed at the time of booking must not be exceeded and all prices must include VAT.

All accommodation providers, irrespective of the size of business, should display the following in the entrance or reception area. In addition, this information must also be displayed outside the premises:

- Current prices of cheapest and most expensive single room.
- Current prices of cheapest and most expensive twin or double room.
- Current prices of cheapest and most expensive family room, i.e. a room for more than two

Figure 4.1. Sample of Classification Criteria.

people, specifying number of people that can be accommodated in each.
- ◆ Prices may be displayed either 'per room' or 'per person'.
- ◆ Prices must be displayed inclusive of VAT.
- ◆ Where a single supplement applies, this must be indicated.

Details of charges, if any, for additional services or facilities available and full details of the establishment's cancellation policy should also be made clear to guests at the time of booking. This includes telephone, fax and email communication, as well as in brochures.

The amenities, facilities and services provided by the establishment, whether by advertisement, brochure, word of mouth or any other means should be described fairly to all visitors and prospective visitors.

Details of any in-house policies, e.g. no smoking, should be communicated at the time of booking. Visitors should be allowed to see the accommodation if they wish before booking.

Prospective guests should be told of any seasonal closure or major refurbishment work in progress. Prospective guests should be confident that their booking has been recorded accurately.

6. Administration
Each visitor should be provided upon request, with details of payments due and a receipt if required. The bill should be clearly presented and well laid out.

7. Statutory obligations
All statutory obligations (and amendments), where applicable, must be met including:

- ◆ **Trade Descriptions Act 1968**. This Act states that it is an offence for you to knowingly or recklessly make 'false statements' about any facility or services offered by you.

- ◆ **The Fire Precautions Act 1971**. This Act stipulates that where accommodation is available for more than six guests and/or staff, or such accommodation is provided above the first floor or below the ground floor, a fire certificate granted by the relevant Fire Authority will usually be required.

- ◆ **The Food Safety Act 1990**. This Act applies to you if you supply food to guests. You must comply with the provisions of the Act. This also applies to the sale of drinks.

- ◆ **The Hotel Proprietors Act 1963**. If this Act applies to your property, a notice must be displayed which limits a hotelier's liability to £50.00 for any article and a maximum of £100.00 per guest (unless deposited for safe keeping).

- ◆ **The Relevant Licensing Act for the country**. If you wish to sell alcohol, you must have a licence to do so. Chapter 6 gives more details regarding this issue.

- ◆ **The Health and Safety Act 1974**. The Act sets the framework for health and safety regulations in the workplace and places responsibilities and duties on all people at work including the employers, the employees and the self-employed.

- ◆ **Disability Discrimination Act 1995**. This Act relates to two aspects of running a business, namely employment of staff and also access to facilities goods and services for the disabled.

- ◆ **Consumer Protection Act 1987**. The Act states that it is a criminal offence for accommodation providers to give guests misleading information on prices charged for accommodation and any related facilities, services or goods.

Figure 4.1. (contd.)

Operators must also maintain Public Liability Insurance Cover. The representative of the inspecting authority may require to see evidence that these requirements are being fulfilled.

8. Access
The proprietor and/or staff should be available generally throughout the day.
Once guests have registered they should have access to the establishment and bedrooms at all times.

9. Advanced ratings
In order to achieve a higher award, additional requirements will have to be met, e.g. to have a four or five-star award.

Grading bands and conditions
The following gives information on the various quality grading levels. This can be found in the scotexchange/BusinessDevelopment website previously mentioned, and then by going to Quality Assurance, Guesthouses, Guidance Notes for Guesthouses and, finally, Grading Bands.

Five Stars	**93 – 100%**
Housekeeping must score	10
No item to score less than	8
All service elements to score excellent	(9 — 10)
Four Stars	**84 – 92%**
Housekeeping not less than	9
No item to score less than	7
50% of total scores to be excellent	(9 — 10)
and 25% of total scores to be very good	(8)
At least 50% of service elements to score excellent	(9 — 10)
Three Stars	**77 – 83%**
Housekeeping not less than	8
No more than two items to score	6
and no more than one of these in any one section	
No acceptable or poor items (less than 6)	
Heating and hospitality sections must not score less than	7
At least 25% of service elements to score excellent	(9 — 10)
Two Stars	**71 – 76%**
Housekeeping not less than	7
No poor items	(less than 3)
Not more than one acceptable item	(less than 6)
and this must not be in the hospitality section	
One Star	**60 – 70%**
Housekeeping not less than	6
No poor items	(less than 3)
Fail – less than 60%	
Below minimum standards	

Figure 4.1. (contd.)

- lighting
- heating
- accessories
- spacious/overall impression.

Each section has an 'ideal' description against which to measure the property. Let us examine the section 'Flooring' and find out how this area would be graded.

Mark 10–9

For example:

High percentage wool-content fitted carpet, professionally laid and in pristine condition. Good thick pile and underlay.

In appropriate establishments, polished boards with high quality occasional mats or rugs.

Mark 8

For example:

High quality thick-pile carpet, beginning to show some flattening. No stains, burns, marks, etc. Carpet with higher percentage of nylon, but in new condition.

Polished boards require buffing, smaller but high quality rugs.

Mark 7–6

For example:

High quality carpet showing flattening in areas of most traffic, but all in sound condition – may be some small discoloration in places. Cheaper new carpet, particularly the more functional and hard wearing.

Polished boards a little scratched in places.

Mark 5–4–3

For example:

Carpets that show considerable use – flattened pile, spots, bleaching by windows, some thinning. Unprofessional fitting – ripples, rough ill-fitting edges thin or no underlay.

There should be no holes, tears, burns or other defects that render the carpet unsound.

Vinyl or low quality flooring with carpet square on top.

Mark 2–1–0

For example:

Where there are distinct signs of wearing – visible canvas, patches, stains, discolouration, obvious seams.

DIY fitting – gaping joints, gaps between carpet and wall.

Several unmatched styles laid patchwork-fashion, or newer carpets laid on top of damaged or worn-through older ones.

Polished boards that are scratched and need a new coat of varnish, with ageing, worn stained rugs.

NB At all levels there may be high quality natural alternatives to carpeting, and in these situations, the intrinsic quality and condition would be assessed in a similar manner, taking into account the style of the property.

The mark level awarded equates to the following:

10 Outstanding
9   Excellent
8   Very good
7   Good
6   Quite good
5   Nearly but not quite good
4   Definitely acceptable
3   Only just acceptable
2   Not quite acceptable
1   Definitely poor
0   Not acceptable

To explain further the quality assurance process, the following is a sample of a fictitious rating for a property. The score for each item is shown with a grading and the comment section gives comments for the proprietor's guidance. It should be pointed out, however, that during the visit to the property, the quality advisor will spend a few hours looking at these aspects and discussing each and every point with the owner. In the grading section above, it can be seen that the rating 79 per cent falls within the three-star rating and so this is the rating that will be awarded to the property at this time. For this property however the

Westover Guest House
Rating: 3 Stars
Overall Score 301/380 (79%)

Exterior	17/20 (85%)
1. Appearance of building	9
2. Grounds and garden	8
Comments: Your building remains excellent and the grounds and tubs are colourful with the bird-feeders a little extra touch for your guests.	

Bedrooms	63/80 (78%)
3. Decoration	8
4. Furnishings and furniture	8
5. Flooring	8
6. Beds, linen, bedding	8
7. Lighting	7
8. Heating	8
9. Accessories	8
10. Spacious/overall impression	8
Comments: Room 2's makeover has been very well done and the new bedding is excellent. The new pine furniture is good and there is still scope to frame the mirrors in a similar wood and add a bit more lighting as discussed. Others rooms are as before but with the quality retained, particularly in the carpets and bedding. New chairs in room 5 will be appreciated by guests.	

Bathrooms and WCs	36/50 (72%)
11. Decoration and flooring	8
12. Fixtures and furniture	7
13. Linen	7
14. Lighting and heating	7
15. Accessories	NA
16. Spaciousness	7
Comments: New tiled sections are very good but monitor sealants. Glad you are keeping to all white tiles. Basic overhead light fittings, in view of what is now available. Small heated towel rail. Good mixer tap shower. As this section will require a level of 77% in future assessments, a further two or three points are necessary and it is suggested that this might be achieved by improvements to lighting, given the wide range of appliances on the market and also improved quality and quantity of towelling.	

Public areas (inc. bar)	43/50 (86%)
17. Decoration	8
18. Fixtures and furniture	8
19. Flooring	10
20. Lighting and heating	9
21. Atmosphere and ambience	8
Comments: Top of the range new carpet and underlay and very neatly fitted especially round the hearth. Older suite has cleaned up well. New scatter cushions. Excellent new lamps with plans for renewal of the overhead lights in due course. Plants add to the atmosphere as does the door being open and the lights on in an evening. Nice art work by local artists.	

Figure 4.2. An example of a quality advisor's assessment.

Dining room	56/70 (80%)
22. Decoration	8
23. Furnishings and furniture	8
24. Flooring	8
25. Lighting and heating	9
26. Menu presentation	8
27. Table appointment	7
28. Atmosphere and ambience	8
Comments: Very much as last visit but with several new lamps to add to atmosphere. Good china but one-ply napkins detract. Well-presented menu. Carpet beginning to show wear and tear. Quality stone detail retained on the fireplace wall.	

Food	14/20 (70%)
29. Dinner – presentation	NA
30. Dinner – quality	NA
31. Breakfast – presentation	7
32. Breakfast – quality	7
Comments: Good selection on the sideboard with portion preserves and butter. Instant coffee. Plentiful grill.	

Hospitality and service	65/80 (81%)
33. Reception – welcome, friendliness, attitude	8
34. Reception – efficiency	7
35. Bedrooms – housekeeping	9
36. Guest bathrooms – housekeeping	9
37. Public areas – housekeeping	9
38. Dining room – housekeeping	9
39. Dining room – dinner service	NA
40. Dining room – breakfast service	8
41. Check-out efficiency	7
Comments: Good telephone contact with directions offered. No actual registration on arrival but met at the car and help with bag offered. Excellent housekeeping throughout with just finer attention needed to sugar bowls and cruet tops. Local papers in lounge is a nice touch. Attentive at breakfast with simple receipt on request.	

Other	7/10 (70%)
42. Tourist information	7
Comments: Standard area Tourist Board packs	

* – Score carried forward

Overall score breakdown

10s: 1	9s: 6	8s: 20	7s: 10	6s: 1	5s: 0
4s: 0	3s: 0	2s: 0	1s: 0	0s: 0	

Figure 4.2. (contd.)

assessment on the bathrooms section shows that the owner has work to do to improve that area, and this has been addressed in the quality advisor's comments for that section. This example is of a fictitious property, which has been a long-time member of the Quality Scheme.

The section on quality assurance seems to have become quite a long section. However, I feel that this is important in order to explain the process carried out by quality advisors. Remember, they are trying to help the operators do well by producing a standard which will be acceptable to the guests. That cannot be bad!

Summary

This chapter has been aimed at helping the reader to understand the concept of quality and, particularly, the fact that quality is related to the needs and wants of the guest within the parameters of the price the guest is prepared to pay. The section that relates to inspections by quality assurance advisors will help you understand how they work so that you can compare your property with a predetermined standard and progress systematically towards it.

The following are the action steps for Chapter 4:

◆ Find out what your customers are looking for.

◆ Decide what you feel you can offer to meet this expectation.

◆ Set your performance standards to meet the expectations.

◆ Plan 'hospitality' routines and checklists.

◆ Create value for money, with possible 'value added'.

◆ Study the requirements of your grading body and evaluate your property against their expectations.

◆ Use the difference to produce a strategic plan for improvements.

CHAPTER FIVE

Reservations and Reception

Reservations

In a small hotel, there is likely to be little need for a highly complex system to maintain reservations and front office information. Having said that, the information kept must be accurate, therefore the system used must achieve this result. Computerised software is available for larger hotels. However, for small hotels up to about twelve rooms, this is overkill.

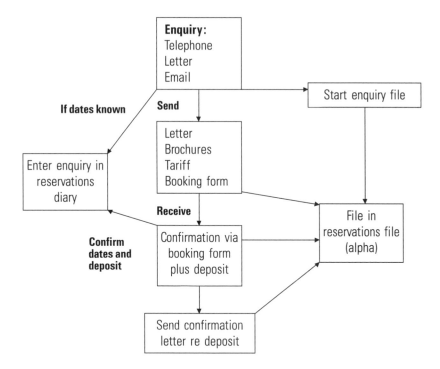

Figure 5. 1. The reservation process.

Procedure for dealing with enquiries

Consider what enquiries you may be faced with, the actions you will need to take and, therefore, the process or system you will need to use.

A guest calls with an enquiry about your property. They may simply want information about what you offer or they may wish to investigate whether you have availability for certain dates.

To cope with this, initially you need to prepare a checklist, which will give you answers to all possible questions. In other words, everything should be at your fingertips. After going through this routine and as you get to know your property, the checklist becomes unnecessary. However, at the beginning, it is useful.

When the call is a general enquiry, give the information and offer to send a brochure and a tariff. For this kind of enquiry, it makes good sense to send something to the enquirer before the sun goes down. Have a standard letter on your computer, which you can personalise, and send this, with the brochure and tariff and possibly even some information about the surrounding area. The guest should feel that they already know something about you and your guesthouse/hotel.

The letter should make the recipient feel warm towards you, the property and the area.

Use a first class stamp since, bear in mind, they might have called other properties and you want to get in first with your information. Check the weight of the information you send to be sure it is within the parameter for first-class post without an excess charge. That would be embarrassing!

If the enquirer is satisfied with the details you give over the telephone and offers you potential dates, first explain the rates and check the dates. If you have space, offer to pencil the reservation in and then send them a brochure, tariff, etc. and a booking form, which they should return to you with a deposit to confirm the reservation. Be sure that your cancellation policy is clearly stated either in the letter or the brochure.

We use a proforma for taking details from the telephone which prompts us to ask questions to ensure we have the necessary details. (See example on p. 69.)

This can be adapted for your own use. When the call is completed, the information should be placed into the appropriate dates within the reservations diary and then the letter produced, confirming the information and the price offered. If you are responding to

Telephone information form

Name:

Address:

Postal code:

Telephone number:

Email address:

Dates required

From:

To:

Number of people:

Double/Twin/Single:

Dinner?

Special needs:

a letter, file it in the enquiry file alphabetically by name. If no letter was received, file the proforma you created while taking the call. The same information should be sent as in the previous enquiry, namely the brochure, tariff, and area brochure. However, a booking form should now be included, and in the letter, you should also ask the guest that they confirm the dates and accommodation requirements by returning the booking form with the required deposit.

Reservations system

The reservations diary is the focal point of the business. It must be kept accurately and must be brought up to date immediately after enquiries and also after the receipt of the booking form and the deposit. Our reservations diary is simply an A4-size desk diary, with a week on a double page, i.e. Monday to Thursday on one page and Friday to Sunday on the opposite one with a space for notes. A day looks like this, taking into consideration that we have six rooms:

Saturday, 28 September		
Room		
1 Double	Thomson	
2 Twin	Sweetnam	Deposit £25.00
3 Double	Lema	
4 Twin/Triple	Rodwell	Deposit £25.00
5 Double		
6 Single		

When an enquiry is made, the name is placed in the diary in pencil as shown with Thomson in room 1 and Lema in room 3, and the brochures etc. are sent out. We are awaiting confirmation. If no response is forthcoming after about three weeks, we may make a call to establish if these potential guests wish to take up the booking or not. This adds to the cost, but if the room has to be released, the earlier the better for the next call coming in.

It is possible to state on the booking form that the tentative reservation will be held until a certain date, but my feeling is that this might create a negative impression in the mind of the guest who might feel you are pushing them for the sake of the deposit.

The bookings in rooms 2 and 4 for Sweetnam and Rodwell are confirmed reservations and deposits have been received as shown. The details here are also in pencil since it is still possible that a cancellation may take place and a change may be necessary.

Rooms 5 and 6 have no notation so they are both available.

Deposit

It is quite usual to request a deposit to hold a booking. The reason for doing this is to obtain a serious commitment from the guest so that they will arrive on the appropriate date. My policy regarding refunding of deposits relates to my approach to maintaining the

---

Booking Form

Westover Guest House
Kilmore

Name:
Address:

Accommodation Required

Twin / Double / Family / Single

Do you wish to have dinner? Yes/No

How many nights?

Reservation Dates: From: To:

I enclose deposit of £   .

Signed:
Date:

Cheques should be made payable to
Westover Guest House

Figure 5.2. Sample booking form.

goodwill of the guest. If a guest calls to cancel a booking and I have a reasonable time to resell, say two weeks, I will happily refund the deposit and write a letter wishing them well with the refund check. If the cancellation is today for tomorrow, I will simply tell the guest that I will refund if I can resell the room, otherwise I will be unable to refund. If I resell the room, I will refund the deposit.

Some kind of policy statement should be made, however, on the brochure and something along the lines of, 'A deposit is requested when booking accommodation. Refunds for cancellation will be made if rooms are re-let for the period or at the discretion of the proprietors'. Remember that you can lose goodwill if this aspect of the business is handled badly. In my opinion, the only time one would not return a deposit would be if the cancellation happened the day before arrival and the room was not re-let.

When a deposit is received from the guest, the notation is made in the reservation book as shown in the example above and the hard copy moves from the enquiry file to the reservation file.

A letter should be sent to the guest confirming the reservation and the receipt of the deposit. Again, this should be an upbeat letter, which states that you are looking forward to meeting them on the date of arrival. If you have an email address, use this and save the cost of postage and letterhead. The guest will also appreciate the promptness of the confirmation that the cheque has arrived.

Collateral materials

You only get one chance to make a good first impression.

Some small properties do not feel the need for a professionally prepared brochure. However, we have had many positive comments about our brochure and we have very few instances where we have sent a brochure which did not convert to a booking. Nowadays, with the excellent software available for computers and the ability to scan in photographs, it is fairly straightforward to produce your own brochure.

The benefit of having a good or professionally prepared brochure lies in the impression you give. Many guests enquire about several properties and when the materials come in, they have the opportunity to compare one with the other. For this reason, it makes good sense to go the professional route.

With the enquiry package, we include a brochure about the local area and our own brochure. For more details about what goes into a brochure, go to Chapter 8 which has information on issues relating to marketing.

Tariff

The tariff should have the guesthouse heading with the address and all contact information, so that if it is detached from the brochure, anyone who finds it knows what it relates to.

Information given should be listed under 'season' months, showing the rates during these periods. If you have differing rates for differing time periods then this should be clearly shown. For example: the rate for one to two nights, for three to six nights and for seven or more nights. The aim of this concept is to encourage guests to book for longer. The financial advantage of a longer stay should be made clear to the guest.

If you have any weekly rates, include them as well as any special packages. Give the price for dinner and explain what dinner means, e.g. three courses and coffee with mints, with a varied selection of choices for each course. Guests may not expect this in a small property, so if you do it, make the information known. Some establishments have sample menus that are reduced in size and which can be included with the tariff.

If you have not included it anywhere else, the cancellation policy can be part of the tariff sheet.

Tariff display

You are obliged to display your tariff for guesthouse residents and for potential guesthouse residents therefore it is wise to have a tariff at the main entrance, which can be seen from the outside. In addition, if you have another door that the guests might approach, i.e. from the car park, then place a tariff there also. Details of the information that should be shown can be found in the quality assurance section of Chapter 4.

Guest registration card

All guests over sixteen years of age are required by law to register with you when they arrive and, after the initial greeting, this is the first order of business. Have the guests give their name, address, including the postal code, and their nationality. It is required that foreign guests should give their passport number and the address of their next destination. In addition, be sure to have the car number recorded. Registration cards must be kept for one year in case they are needed for any kind of police investigation. The relevant legislation is the Immigration (Hotel Records) Order of 1972.

Many companies produce relatively inexpensive professional registration forms and you will receive solicitation to buy such items from time to time in the usual array of unsolicited mail you will receive.

Guest history

At this stage, as you are gaining information about your guests, you may wish to consider starting a guest history. This can be computerised in the form of a database or it can be a rotary type of file on which you build up details of information about your guests, which will help you to serve them better and show that you have a 'memory' of them.

It would start with the names and address of the guest, and then provide an ongoing record of their stays with you and any additional information you glean which will help you serve them better. For example, if on the first visit they enjoyed being in guest room 3, make a note and if they call again, if possible offer that room again. If you know of birth dates or anniversary dates, record them and cross-reference them to the reservations diary and send a card at the appropriate time.

If there are dietary issues, record them and plan for this on their next stay. If they requested feather-free pillows, make sure they are available and when talking to them, when they call, you can be the one to mention it and they will be impressed. In some ways, this is why a rotary file, next to the telephone, is a good idea.

Introducing the guest to the property

In Chapter 4 under the hospitality section I suggested to you a process for making the guest feel welcome to your property and for them to get to know you and vice versa. In addition to this friendly and informal introduction to the property, there should be a more precise yet conversational induction to the property during which time your 'house rules' as well as useful information can be transmitted.

Key to this might be a folder, which you have prepared and placed in the guest room. This will give local information about places to see, things to do, etc. In addition, will be the 'in-house' information. This will include items such as:

◆ Meal times and any possible exception or special arrangement that can be made.

◆ Special services such as packed lunch, availability of irons, hair dryers, etc.

◆ Special information such as confirmation of a 'no smoking' policy.

◆ How to use the telephone and telephone charges per unit including the time for a unit based on local and long distance calls.

◆ Fire regulations and what to do in an emergency. This must be detailed on the back of the bedroom door. Give information if you are likely to hold a fire drill.

◆ List of acceptable methods of payment.

◆ Laundry or drying facilities if applicable.

Bills

In large hotels, the guest bill or folio is retained in the cashier's area at the front desk and as the guest incurs any charges within the hotel, the details are quickly taken to the front desk for posting to the folio. Speed is important, particularly in the morning, to be sure that charges are posted before the guest checks out. Some hotels have a computerised link from each revenue centre which adds the charge to the folio directly as it is made at the remote point in the hotel.

Given the limited services in a small hotel or guesthouse, coupled with the closeness of you, the operator, to everything that is going on, the guest billing process need not be excessively complex.

It is important to record any sales which are made on a day-to-day basis, to be sure that these charges are included on the final bill that you will give to the guest on the morning of departure. Since you or your spouse/partner are likely to be involved in all sales the compilation of the final bill should not pose a major problem.

Our system is simple in that I keep a ledger in the bar and, by date, I make a record of any dinners, drinks or wine served each evening. It has the following detail:

◆ Date
◆ Name
◆ Room number
◆ Dinners served
◆ Dinners charge in £
◆ Drinks served
◆ Drinks charge in £

- Wine served
- Wine charge in £
- Total charge for this date

Some guests may wish to pay cash as they consume the drinks, so it is wise to have a small float in the bar to facilitate the giving of change.

The bill template, which we use, has on it:

Letterhead information

- To: (guest name)
- Date
- X nights bed and breakfast per person = (total charge)
- X dinners served = (total charge)
- Bar items – see detail overleaf = (total charge)
- Wine served – see detail overleaf = (total charge)
- Telephone charges – see detail overleaf = (total charge)
- Any other charges
- Total charge
- Less deposit
- Final total

Thank you for staying at XXX and we look forward to welcoming you back again.

Figure 5.3. Sample bill.

This is not rocket science, and it could be improved by having the template in the computer, details inserted in the computer and then printed off. We do not do that. We keep it homely and hand-write it with the list of drinks, wines or telephone calls on the back of the bill. This is made up the night before departure. You need to check in the morning for telephone calls, although in this day and age, most calls are by mobile so that is now hardly an issue.

If you wish to be more formal, it is possible to purchase printed, duplicate bills, which enable you to include details of your property, and then have space for the different heading similar to the above bill. In addition, in the width of the page, it is possible to have seven days with the dates above each day and the daily detail of charges included. The amounts again, however, are hand entered. Purchased bills are more costly than self-prepared bills but they are probably more professional.

The duplicate aspect of the bill means that you have retained the information for accounting references and in case of requests for information from the Inland Revenue.

Receipts

It is necessary to give guests a receipt for any monies received and this can be done by having a separate receipt book which simply lists the date, received £XX from (guest name) and signed by you. If you use the bill mentioned above, which is duplicated, you can simply write across the bill, 'Received from Mr XX the sum of £ XX' and then sign the bill. The duplicate copy is the receipt you have created.

Guest book

Finally, it is a nice touch to have a guest book in which guests are free to make any comments. It is something many guests want to do and they enjoy reading other guests' comments. Foreign guests particularly seem keen to leave something behind in the form of a comment. Perhaps more importantly, it is good for your ego when they show their appreciation!

Summary

This chapter suggested one workable system for reservations, reception and guest billing. There are many others available, including computerised software systems. What is important is that the system is not too time consuming, but is very accurate.

The following are the action steps for Chapter 5:

◆ Develop your reservation and booking process.
◆ Create a procedure for handling enquiries.
◆ Prepare a question prompt proforma for gathering guest information.

◆ Decide on a reservations system.

◆ Create a booking form.

◆ Produce a tariff form separate from the brochure.

◆ Display tariff outside and inside property.

◆ Plan to develop a guest history record.

◆ Produce or purchase guest registration cards.

◆ Plan a guest orientation checklist.

◆ Produce information for guest room folder.

◆ Decide on a guest bill format or order pre-prepared guest bills.

◆ Decide on your process for giving guests receipts.

CHAPTER SIX

Food and Beverage

Your experience

How far you go into the food side of your business will depend on your experience as a chef and, while an enthusiastic amateur can produce good meals, some professional experience is certainly useful in order to meet the requirements of your guests. Here, I am referring to having good kitchen organisation as well as culinary ability.

It is important to remember that you need to give your customers what they want, not what you think they would like to have. This may cause you some disappointment since you might be a tremendous producer of Indian food, but if that is not what the guests want, you will not sell any food, and letting rooms might become more difficult.

Breakfast and breakfast menus

> In a guest house, one of the key 'memory' factors is the breakfast you offer.

Many properties let themselves down by simplifying the service and minimising the cost by producing a pre-prepared, low-cost fixed breakfast plate. We have found that not only does such a procedure disappoint, but that it may even be wasteful and therefore expensive. Many guests are only interested in a hot drink and maybe toast. If you have a pre-prepared dish, which has to be thrown out, the cost is yours.

The menu is important, as is cooking to order, so that each guest obtains a freshly prepared meal other than a few items that can be cooked slightly in advance. Figure 6.1 shows a standard and fairly acceptable menu, but you must decide what you want to offer. This decision will be based upon the prices you charge, your technical ability and what you think the customers want. If you have a high rate for B&B, with higher guest expectations,

Breakfast Menu

Choice of:
Orange Juice, Grapefruit Juice, Cranberry Juice
Fresh Half Grapefruit or Stewed Prunes
Fresh Fruit Plate by Arrangement

Porridge, Corn Flakes, Frosties, Healthwise Bran Flakes, Alpen Muesli

Grilled Loch Fyne Kippers
Poached Smoked Haddock

Eggs Any Style – Fried, Poached, Scrambled, Boiled
Grilled Smoked Back Bacon
Grilled Pork Sausages
Scottish Black Pudding
Fried Potatoes or Potato Scone
Grilled Tomato
Fried Mushrooms

Toast, Oatcakes, Bread Rolls

Tea, Coffee, Hot Chocolate, Assortment of Herb Teas

Figure 6.1. A standard breakfast menu.

then the menu will be more extensive, possibly with higher quality items. Occasionally one finds menus with items such as 'Creamy Scrambled Eggs with Smoked Salmon Strips', 'Devilled Lamb Kidneys', 'Kedgeree', and the like. Such a menu, of course, means more preparation, higher cost items and increased potential for waste.

The standard menu shown above virtually eliminates waste and generally satisfies the guests. In order to prevent waste, when you have guests with you for some time, remember what they order and prepare accordingly. While some guests change their order daily, the majority are creatures of habit, so you can generally predict fairly well what they will order.

The only items to be precooked will be the sausages and the tomatoes. The sausages can be grilled just before service and can be kept in the oven in a covered container with the tomatoes, which will cook gradually. The covered container retains the moistness. The bacon can be grilled in batches as the orders are taken, and all eggs should be prepared to order. Remember that after the order is taken, the guest will, in most cases, have their fruit juice and then cereal, so there is an element of preparation time available. In city centre hotels, where you are dealing with business guests who might be rushing to work, perhaps more advance preparation will be necessary.

Guesthouses and small hotels have an advantage over large hotels in that it is possible to cook to order. Large hotels often have an extensive buffet with virtually everything pre-prepared and a real potential for waste.

Breakfast checks and pre-ordering

Some guesthouses ask guests to order breakfast the night before on pre-prepared order slips. These are a bit like the room service orders found in hotels for breakfast, giving details and the time required. While this definitely avoids waste, my own feeling is that it does not really give the level of service I want to offer my guests.

Dinner and the dinner menu

Decision on the dinner offered will relate to technical ability, the price the guest is prepared to pay, and the kind of menu they would prefer to have. Again, I stress that you should try to establish the needs, wants and expectations of your guests and not try to force upon them what you want to prepare.

Some establishments offer simple fare such as a dish of the day and a home-made soup. In many cases this is acceptable to the guests. However, if you have up to six or eight guests who want dinner, finding one dish that all will be happy with, may be a challenge.

Our decision was to give good choices, cook items relatively simply but to specialise on serving a broad selection of fresh vegetables. This is our 'wow' factor and it works well for us. Our dinner menu, shown in Figure 6.2 falls into three sections.

We use a number of purchased dessert items, which are 'freezer' items. Many are of excellent quality and are well accepted by guests and they supplement the 'home-made' items we prepare ourselves. We decorate and add our own personal touch using sauces and fresh fruit.

Starters

1. A home-made soup, e.g. Lentil, Carrot & Coriander, Mushroom, etc.
2. A salad type or fruit dish, e.g. Caesar Salad, Apple Salad, Melon & Orange Cocktail, Melon Boat.
3. A hot starter with salad garnish, e.g. Salmon Cakes, Crab Cakes, Quiche.
4. A 'meaty' salad, e.g. Salad Nicoise, Egg Mayonnaise, Home-made Pâté & Oatcakes, Smoked Trout, Smoked Mackerel & Horseradish Sauce.

Main Courses

1. A pan-fried fish dish, e.g. Pan-Fried Salmon, Pan-Fried Trout, Breaded Cod.
2. A meat dish, e.g. Pork Medallions with Orange Sauce, Braised Steak or Venison, Grilled Lamb Cutlets, Gammon Steak, Pork Chop with Apple Sauce.
3. A poached chicken dish, e.g. with Tomato & Basil Sauce, Mushroom Sauce etc.

Desserts

1. A home made 'homely' item, e.g. Rhubarb & Apple Crumble, Apple Pie, Zucchini & Pineapple Cake.
2. A hot fruit, e.g. Poached Peaches or Pears.
3. A fruit item, e.g. Banana Split, Peach Melba, Bananas Cooked in Rum.
4. A 'freezer' item, e.g. Key Lime Pie, Black Forest Gateaux, Crème Caramel.

Figure 6.2. Our dinner menu.

Offering multiple choices for each course requires some cooking ability, but most importantly, it requires good organisational skills and the best use of the equipment available. More about menu planning related to available equipment later.

My wife and I are not qualified chefs. However, I did attend hotel school and had cookery classes, but that was not yesterday, and by no stretch of the imagination could either of us be called chefs. In Chapter 3, I introduced a daily work schedule for both of us. As far as dinner is concerned, however, I prepare the foods for dinner in the afternoon. In the evening, I serve the food and my wife cooks the main dishes and vegetables. I prepare all the starters pre-service other than the hot ones, which she does, and we both put together the desserts. I prepare the coffees. This works very well for us.

The key to this, however, is having the dinner order for starter and main dish in advance. Since it is a small guesthouse, we feel it is acceptable to get the orders in advance, and we do this by having the dinner menu available at breakfast time. The guests who are having dinner seem happy to order the starter and main dish in the morning.

When guests have arrived and are settled into their rooms, we show them the dinner menu and ask them their selections. What this means is that, generally, we have all the information we need by 6.00p.m. and this gives us time to be well prepared for the start of dinner service at 7.00p.m.

An important factor relating to the evolution of our menu, to some extent through trial and error, was making use of all the equipment available to us in the kitchen, without overloading any one piece of equipment and thereby causing a timing problem. Some of the vegetables are prepared on top of the stove, some in a steamer and some in the oven. For the main dishes, we have chicken, which is poached on top of the stove, pan-fried fish on top of the stove, oven-prepared items and also grilled items.

If you have experience of presentation of food, this is good. If not, look at photographs in cookery books and magazines, and experiment. Be artistic. Get six main dish garnishes, which you practise and perfect and use them on different dishes. Gradually build up your repertoire of garnishes and sauces. Later in this chapter in the section on service, I have mentioned that possibly the simplest method is to use plated service. However you can choose serving dishes and serve the food, or even family-type service by placing the service dishes on the table and letting the guests serve themselves.

Our menu is planned on a daily basis and as well as paying attention to variety for longer term guests, we always make sure there is a good spread of the use of the equipment. You can, however, have a pre-planned cyclical menu which runs for a period, maybe eight days and then starts all over again. Try to avoid a seven-day menu which means that Monday night is the venison steak night!

Menu planning

There are a number of aspects which must be taken into consideration when planning a menu. The following chart helps to put them into perspective.

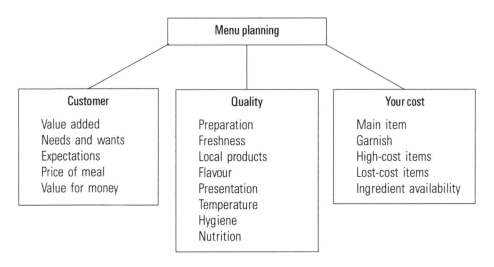

Figure 6.3 Planning a menu.

In analysing this chart, one can see that menu planning must recognise the customer's wants, as I have stressed numerous times. When they read the menu, it should be a pleasant surprise, and you know you have done well when they tell you they are 'spoiled for choice.' In addition, what they see should match their expectations in terms of the price to be charged. Having had the meal, they should feel that what they had was value for money and that they have been well served by the menu.

In order to satisfy these needs, quality aspects should be taken into account. One must consider the adequacy of the preparation. It must be well prepared to be accepted, so the cook/chef must be able to get it right first time and every time. When planning a menu, practise the items to be sure they can be produced well time after time.

Ingredients must be fresh and in good condition. Flavouring should be checked and the presentation on the plate should be attractive, contrasting and colourful. Hot items should be served hot, and cold items cold. The plates should be hot for hot dishes.

While it is not necessary to be a nutritionist, we must remember that our guests are aware of nutritional issues and we must stay abreast of the latest trends and even fads to be sure we are meeting our guest's expectations. In addition, we must be aware of issues relating to allergic reactions to some foods such as nuts and certain shellfish, and to issues of guests who have problems like lactose intolerance, or gluten intolerance with the need for a gluten-free diet, as well as the needs of people such as diabetics. If you advertise that you cater for special diets, then you must be prepared for this. Most guests give good warning of their needs, and generally make suggestions to help you plan for their meals.

Hygiene is an issue which is of vital importance and a separate section on this will appear later in this chapter.

Profit is not a dirty word and our aim is to make a profit while satisfying the guest's price/value need. Costing the menu, particularly the dinner menu, is most important. Generally speaking, the main dish item will be the highest cost and this should be costed accurately so that you know what garnish you can use to even out the cost. For example an Aberdeen Angus 10oz sirloin steak, coupled with fresh asparagus tips, might put the costing over the top. It is important to remember, however, that one item might have a high cost while another item has a lower cost. If you sell four steaks and at the same time sell four chicken breasts, which are considerably less expensive, then the average costing might well be acceptable and the menu, with the steaks on it, is impressive.

In order to give greater variety and bring in some additional revenue, it may be possible to offer supplementary menu items at an additional charge on a set menu. For example, you might have smoked salmon as a starter for £2.00 additional charge, over and above the fixed price.

I mentioned earlier that we use some frozen dessert items, which are of high quality and, provided there is sufficient choice, this generally seems acceptable to guests. Major frozen food suppliers now produce high quality pre-prepared foods which are simply reheated, and this might be an answer if cooking skills are not yet honed to perfection. Such items are, however, quite expensive and while the guests are likely to be very satisfied with the quality of the product, if the charge is too high, the price/value aspect will be compromised. If you do not charge enough, the guests will be happy but your accountant might not be.

Menu design

One of the nicest menus I have ever seen was for a very exclusive small hotel, which prided itself on local produce and game. The surround of the menu was an excellent piece of art in which the artist had filled the area with fruits, vegetables and game items in the foreground, with the fields and hills in the background. The colours were vibrant and the presentation was most attractive.

Without going to this extreme, most print shops sell paper which is framed, and many designs are possible. You can also buy software which can help you to produce your own designs if you wish.

There are a few straightforward rules to take into consideration when setting up a menu:

♦ Make sure the type is big enough to be read, especially if your guests are mainly older people!

♦ Try to avoid a coloured background or decorative background which makes it difficult to read the menu.

♦ Make it big enough so that it does not look squeezed into a small area.

♦ The decision is yours whether you use French or not, but if you do, have good descriptions in English. Know what your guests would expect and do not take the chance of embarrassing them. Even if it is in English, describe things well without the use of kitchen terms, e.g. demi-glace, jus lie, concasse etc. People do not know what they mean!

♦ There are many descriptive fonts available on most computers, but try to use a bold one for easy reading rather than a very fine one.

♦ If menus are reused, check on every use to be sure that they are in good condition and not decorated with ketchup and raspberry jam.

♦ If you use framed paper, know the lead-time for re-ordering so that you do not run out.

I have seen many different menu-holders, including a wooden one that weighted about 1.5 kilos and could barely be lifted. If you want to have a cover, have one that fits with the dining room décor and which can be easily handled. Consider the concept of tabloid newspapers as against broadsheets and make the menu easy to handle, particularly on a small table.

Breakfast menus are not likely to change a great deal so consider having them laminated. Breakfast is a messy meal and the laminated menu can be wiped off with a damp cloth after each use.

Food and beverage control

In this book, I have spoken a lot about satisfying customers' needs but you must never lose sight of the fact that profit is important to you also. You have to juggle with the price/value issue and the profit issue. The key to profit in food and beverage operation is creating and applying time after time, effective standards. Standards relate to many areas as shown in the following points.

◆ **Purchase specifications**. What this means is that your purchasing should be coordinated and planned so that you buy the same quality, size and weight of item every time you buy it. This means firstly, vetting the supplier to be sure the quality is consistently there, and then making sure the portion size you buy is consistent. Remember, that if the portion of salmon fillet is too small, the guest is dissatisfied. If it is too large, your profit is reduced. Get it right time after time.

◆ **Portion size.** Establish the portion size as part of a standard recipe and be sure that you achieve that portion size time after time. This also applies to drink measures if you serve alcohol and bear in mind that it is necessary to use legal sized measures for all drinks. Think about when you are serving a cola to a guest. Let's say you decide that your portion is eight fluid ounces and therefore for the price you charge you serve the drink in a filled eight fluid ounce glass. If a staff member does not know what the portion is, they might use a pint glass, i.e. 20 fluid ounces. You can see the problem. You need to establish the portion size, communicate it to all concerned and supply the right equipment. This also applies in relation to food items and the equipment you use to portion food, e.g. perforated spoons, scoops and even single portion dishes, should be the right size. In addition, if the main dish plate size is too big, there is a tendency to fill it. The result might be leftover food, since the portion size is too big. That waste on the plate, which goes in your swill bin, is your profit being thrown out.

◆ **Recipes**. Initially, you should come up with a list of starters, main dishes and desserts that you feel you will offer. If you have a menu, which changes daily and guests who have relatively long stays, then you need quite a variety of dishes. It is important that you develop standard recipes so that every time you produce the dish, it is the same. More importantly, the menu item which you had calculated to produce an acceptable profit, will be produced the same every time, giving you the same profit. Standard recipes will generally show ingredients, quantities, cooking temperature and times, preparation method, and information regarding the presentation and garnish. Remember that if you substitute a more expensive garnish, the profit reduces. Experiment with recipes to be sure you can cook them, to visually check that it is pleasing to the eye and to gauge acceptability to your guests. When you get it right, produce it that way every time. Remember that an acceptable dish will have the right mix of colour, taste, texture, aroma and flavour.

◆ **Recipe costing**. When you have created a recipe that you will use, list the recipe's ingredients and cost out each one. Total the cost and then you know what it costs to produce. If the recipe and portion size is repeated time after time, then the costing will remain the same, unless the unit price of any of the ingredients increases. If this does happen and you do not increase the price to your customers, you take on the reduction in profit. In truth, it is unlikely you will increase prices when all your advertising has shown your current prices. Realistically what restaurant groups do is try to plot a middle cost for a period and recognise that they will make more profit in the first half of the year and less in the second half.

Ongoing cost control

When I started off in this industry, particularly on the food and beverage side of it, control was of great importance, as it is now, but it was certainly managed less efficiently than it is in this day and age. We used to take stock on a monthly basis and then calculate the cost of materials (foodstuffs) and work out a food cost percentage (as a percentage of sales for the same period) by about the middle of the following month. If things had gone badly wrong during the period, you worked in the dark for about six or seven weeks before you found out the dreaded news that you were losing money.

When I was running a group of restaurants, I upset my staff greatly by asking for a weekly stocktaking in order to obtain the information faster. By Tuesday afternoon, I knew the result for the previous week. This allowed me to act quickly in case of a problem and made it easier to identify the cause of the problem.

Nowadays most hotel or restaurant companies calculate a daily food cost percentage so that in the morning, you know what happened yesterday. One aspect of this system, however, is that it is based on purchases and sales for the day and does not reflect the daily changes in the level of the stock. This does, however, become less of an issue as the month goes on and the cumulative figures begin to even out the stock fluctuations.

In a small hotel or guesthouse, control is very much in the hands of the owners, and if you are the only 'workers' then control is simplified. For your interest and as an ongoing control of food, alcoholic beverage and wine cost, this can be fairly easily calculated, taking only a few minutes every day. To begin with, you need a target. This can be complex. However, in the following section, I will explain a simple method of working out a cost percentage target.

Let us assume that on your breakfast menu, you take an average meal, which is shown in Figure 6.4 below, and then apply the individual cost to calculate the average cost of a breakfast. Some people will have more for breakfast that this, some will take less, but we have to try to calculate an average. A more accurate method would be to establish the actual usage over, for example, two weeks to identify the true average, but this exercise will give you a reasonable average cost.

Item	Cost
Orange juice	10p
Cornflakes	19p
Egg	07p
Bacon	14p
Sausage	09p
Tomato	07p
Coffee, milk, etc.	06p
Toast	02p
Butter	03p
Marmalade	12p
Total cost	89p

Figure 6.4. Cost of an average breakfast.

It is necessary for you to decide on the sales price for breakfast, and so you must make the decision on that and stick with it. Let's assume that you charge £25.00 for bed and breakfast. What do you want the sales price for breakfast to be? Let's decide on £3.50 so that the accommodation element is £21.50. We will come back to this again, after we have calculated an average food cost for dinner.

The dinner calculation is more complex. The process is the same in that you cost out each item and then try to decide on an average cost. As with breakfast, the most accurate method would be to take a test period and calculate the dinner cost for that period, and then make an average dinner cost by dividing the total cost by the number of dinners served. I suggest simplifying this by costing each menu item and then calculating an average starter, main dish, dessert and coffee.

Item	Cost		
Tomato & Basil Soup	32p		
Smoked Trout (with garnish)	£1.14		
Apple Salad	58p		
Egg Mayonnaise	45p	Average	62p
Salmon Fillet (Potato & Veg)	£1.48		
Gammon Steak ''	£1.32		
Poached Chicken Breast etc.	84p	Average	£1.21
Fruit Crumble & Custard	75p		
Bread & Butter Pudding	£1.22		
Strawberry Meringue	£1.15		
Blackcurrant Cheesecake	£1.05	Average	£1.04
Coffee & Mints	47p	Average	47p
Average dinner cost	£3.34		

Figure 6.5. Cost of an average dinner.

Sales mix is of course a factor, which a more accurate costing would take into account. However, for the sake of this calculation based on a small property, the above is a reasonable target. For this calculation, let's say dinner sells for £15.00.

If you intend to apply this method of control over a period of a month, and at the end of the month, you calculate that you have served 280 breakfasts and 160 dinners, then the target for that month of food cost percentage would be calculated using the formula in Figure 6.6 below.

	Sold	Average cost	Total cost	Sales value	
Breakfast served	280	89p	£249.20	£980.00	(£3.50)
Dinners served	160	£3.34	£855.04	£2,400.00	(£15.00)
Totals			£1,104.24	£3,380.00	

$$\frac{\text{Food cost} \times 100}{\text{Food sales} \times 1}$$

$$\frac{1104.24 \times 100}{3380.00 \times 1}$$

Food cost % = 32.7%

Figure 6.6. Budgeted food cost percentage.

This, then, has calculated for you a theoretical average food cost percentage. Now, on a daily basis, you can calculate the actual cost to see how you are doing.

To do this, create a chart similar to the one below and then enter the information. The 'cost today' column is the cost of food purchased. The 'cumulative cost' is the ongoing cost as the month progresses. The 'sales today' column is the sales, calculated using the numbers sold times the £3.50 for breakfast and the £15.00 for dinner.

The cumulative food cost percentage is calculated using the formula we used above, i.e. the cumulative cost over the cumulative sales, times 100 over 1, gives you the cumulative food cost percentage, as shown in Figure 6.7. If your costs are high today because you have bought a lot of food which will be used over the next few days, the cost percentage will be negatively affected. However, it will average out as the month progresses.

Date	Cost Today	Cost Cum.	Sales Today	Sales Cum.	Cum. %
May 1	25	25	75	75	33%
May 2	35	60	90	165	36%
May 3	50	110	120	285	39%
May 4	30	140	105	390	36%

Figure 6.7. Daily and cumulative food cost percentage.

This can be checked if you wish by taking the inventories at the beginning and end of the month and using the formula:

opening stock + purchases — closing stock = cost of food consumed

The same formula can be applied to calculate the actual food cost percentage using the cost and sales figures.

Note that this will be affected by staff meals and also any waste that takes place during the period. If the cost is high and you know you have had waste, then the control is working to tell you to eliminate waste.

The same process can be used to calculate the bar and the wine percentage.

Purchasing

I have emphasised the need for effective purchasing a number of times. To some extent, depending on location, your choices may be limited and you may have to rely on a weekly or twice weekly delivery from a wholesaler. In this case, you would need to plan menus and purchase accordingly, taking into account the number of guests anticipated. Alternatively, you may be able to choose between a number of local suppliers, including the wholesaler, the local cash and carry, specialists like the fishmonger, butcher and greengrocer and, last but not least, the supermarket.

The aim of purchasing is to buy the right product at the right price, at the right quality and from the right supplier.

The first thing to do is to check out the suppliers. You have a responsibility to serve wholesome and safe food to your guests and you have to be sure in your mind that your suppliers have the same objective. Do not be afraid to visit the premises and get a feel for their attention to detail, cleanliness and hygiene.

When you are satisfied, look into the range of products offered and consider this in relation to your plans for your menu. Next, check the prices per item or unit price and see if this is compatible with the prices you are charging. Is one supplier expensive? Does the less expensive supplier supply the quality you are looking for?

If you are dealing with a wholesaler, get to know their catalogue of products thoroughly. Initially, the glossy pictures may help you with your menu planning. Learn the prices so that when there is a price change, you are aware of it. Remember that an increase to you, which is not compensated for by an increase in your selling price, means reduced profit.

When dealing with a cash and carry store, get to know your way around. Get acquainted with the department heads and do not be afraid to ask what specials are available on a given day. Let the butchery department know that you are interested in their specials and when they see you, they will offer them. Often, specials are items that are getting close to 'display by' dates and the decision is yours whether you buy and use them but, if you can include them in a menu immediately, there should be no problem.

If you have one of the leading supermarkets in your locality, there is a possibility again of getting to know section heads and being offered bargains. Remember that you are likely to be visiting on a daily basis and you become known by the staff. When they know what you are looking for, they are likely to look out for you when they have specials that they know you generally buy.

Remember also that most supermarkets have a 'loss leader' policy, which means that they sell certain items at less than cost to attract the customers. Since you will get to know the store well, you will spot the loss leaders and you can take advantage of them. Supermarkets often have wine sales also, which offer a 20 per cent discount and sometimes five per cent off if you buy six bottles. Look out for such offers and compare the prices with your local cash and carry. You may be pleasantly surprised.

Where possible, I want to help my local community and so I will use local, individual suppliers like butchers and fishmongers if I can, but only if the quality and price is right. It is acceptable to ask for a business discount and if this brings the price down to that of the wholesaler or the supermarket, then it is helpful to buy from them as long as the quality is right.

Earlier, we discussed the ability or experience you bring to your business in relation to the purchasing process, in that you may make the decision to buy pre-prepared or convenience items for use in the dinner menu. Such items are generally of a very high quality.

There are two issues to consider, however. The first is that those items are generally quite expensive, and cost more than purchasing the ingredients from scratch and preparing them. Another consideration here, however, is that with convenience items, there is likely to be no waste. Generally, though it is likely that purchased pre-prepared items will reduce profit unless you can increase prices accordingly.

The second issue is that guests who eat out quite a bit may well recognise the pre-prepared items and therefore know that the cooking is not home cooking. Having said that, if the food item is high quality, it may well be very acceptable to your guests. As previously mentioned, adding your own personal touch can disguise the basic commodity and make it very acceptable.

One other point to be mentioned about receiving purchases is to check that you have received what you ordered at the price you ordered at, and that the quantities received agree with the quantities stated on the invoice.

Storage of food and liquor

In a small property, you will not be likely to carry a large stock of food and liquor. However, there are some points to bear in mind. You should have enough refrigerator and freezer space to hold the items you are likely to need to carry at your busiest time, taking into consideration that there should be space for air circulation within the equipment.

Dry goods should be kept in a storage area on shelves which have smooth, impervious surfaces and which are easy to clean. Nothing should be stored on the floor as this hampers cleaning. Dry products such as bulk flour, sugar, etc. should be kept in containers with tight-fitting lids.

All items in stores should be rotated, with new items going to the back and old ones coming forward for immediate use.

Liquor should, if possible, be kept in a separate store, which is kept secure and locked at all times. It is sad to relate but unprotected liquor has a tendency to walk and so the simple precaution of a lockable area is advised. If you have staff and a key holder who has responsibility for the liquor store area leaves, it makes sense to change the lock. This is not such an expensive process as might be thought as it is only necessary to replace the tumblers to change the mechanism, which will then require a different key.

Kitchen equipment

There are a number of factors to consider when purchasing kitchen equipment:

- Do you really need it?
- Of the equipment available, what will be most efficient taking into consideration the planned menu?
- How often will it be used?
- How much space does it take up?
- How easy is to clean?
- How durable is it (e.g. plastic versus stainless steel)?
- How safe is it to use?
- What is the cost to buy and to run?
- Should it be gas or electric?
- Is it better to buy one large or two small? (operating costs during slack periods).
- Are repairs and replacement parts readily available?
- Do we buy new or used?

Chances are that in a small property, the kitchen will be little more than a domestic kitchen. While it is possible to work within these constraints, you should be considering what changes you might make when replacements need to be made, or you may have a plan to change the equipment piece by piece over a period of time.

Our kitchen is a domestic kitchen. However, we have augmented the equipment with certain items to improve what we can offer on our menu. In our first year, we replaced an oven with a double oven/grill and our next improvement will be a more comprehensive hob area. In addition, we have purchased some light equipment, which makes our job somewhat easier.

There are a few things worth mentioning when considering buying light equipment, which you may or may not need. Firstly, it takes up space. Secondly if not used frequently, it gets dusty and greasy, and thirdly, if used frequently, it means additional items to be washed as part of the process of serving a meal. To give an example, my wife decided to buy an egg poacher unit to standardise the poached eggs. However, what that means is that instead of a pot and a perforated spoon to wash and dry, i.e. two items, there is in addition, the five-piece egg poacher which fits into the pot. How many bread-making machines have you seen on the top shelves of friends' kitchens, having only been used once? Perhaps you have one yourself! It is also worth considering whether you can reduce the catering skills needed through the equipment you buy. There are quite a number of pieces of kitchen equipment on the market which are successful every time you use them and reduce or eliminate cooking skills. Bread makers, julienne cutters, crêpe makers and grooved griddles are included in this category.

The same applies to the use of convenience foods, as has been mentioned.

Dining room equipment

There is not such a great deal of equipment required in the dining room. It depends on the style you wish to present. Other than the usual tables and chairs, it may be useful to have a wine and beer refrigerator, assuming of course that no draught beer is being served. Most bars will have optics for the measurement of spirits, and these should be the size required by the licensing law. You also need fixed bottle openers for beer bottles and wine openers for wine as well as coolers for white and rosé wines and baskets for red wines.

It is quite common to have a buffet for fruits, juices and cereals for breakfast service and a sideboard is useful since plates and cereals can be kept inside it during the day.

You may wish to have a coffee machine in the dining room, which also heats water for tea making. Be sure the temperature of the hot water is adequate to make decent tea. This would save constant trips to the kitchen for tea and coffee during both breakfast and dinner service. This is an example of an expense which has the benefit of saving your energy.

Food service

A decision has to be made on what style of food service you wish to have. It depends on your ability, or that of your staff. If you want to have Entrecôte Dianne and Crêpes Suzette, which are prepared in the dining room, remember that everyone else in the dining room will have to wait while you are tied up with that. Consider also the smoke and heat detectors!

Nouvelle Cuisine and Cuisine Moderne have taken us down the route of the beautifully decorated plate, and so plate service is the 'in thing'. This is possibly the ideal route to go in that it results in a need for the least amount of equipment and less work and washing up!

You also have to make decisions about the style of your dining room. Will it be separate tables or a refectory style table for all? Tablecloths, table mats or just bare wood? How do the tables look without cloths? Is dinner service more a white tablecloth, candlelit event, or a bare table?

How about breakfast? Is that to be less formal, and so is the bare table or the table mat acceptable?

To some extent, the answer to all these questions relates to the image you wish to create and also the price/value issue we have spoken of in Chapter 4.

We have checked table toppers on a pink base cloth for breakfast and the same pink bases with white tablecloths for dinner. For breakfast, we use three-ply paper napkins, and for dinner we use linen napkins. We use regular glass for breakfast juices, but all glassware for dinner is crystal. I mention what we do simply to offer options and to show how you can mix and match.

Consider also the cutlery and crockery you wish to use. It should be in keeping with the establishment and the price charged. Stainless steel might be acceptable, or you may decide to go with silver plate. Crockery can be fine china or chunky pottery depending on the style of your property, but remember that it should be dishwasher safe and consider also the durability factor. Remember that chunky, durable plates tend to be heavy and this might be a factor if you have to carry them a long way to and from the dining room. Look at auctions since sometimes you can obtain large sets of a nice pattern of quality tableware for a good price.

A word on the physical aspect of serving food. It is hard work, and the inexperienced server will find they are developing muscles where they did not know they had body parts! If your previous job was a sedentary one, you will know by now that this one is not. The key is to 'work smart and not hard' and this translates into developing good routines. Always be prepared and think ahead about all the tools and equipment you will need before service. By doing this, you will not be running back and forward for single items. Use a tray to carry multiple items before service and so reduce journeys.

Before you walk from the dining room to the kitchen, look around the room and see if there is anything you can take with you. Is there a table that can be cleared?

Do the same when coming from the kitchen to the dining room. Never walk with empty hands. Advanced preparation, is the key to being effective in this business.

Learn also how to bend down, for example when you unload the dishwasher. If you pick up a couple of plates at a time, you will be up and down numerous times. Bend the knees and lift all items out to a surface above and next to the dishwasher and then get up and store them. This will avoid backache.

Entertainment

If you have live music or play taped music or CDs, then the Performing Rights Society and Phonographic Performances Ltd will be interested in you and you will be required to apply for a licence. You need a licence from the Performing Rights Society if you play any copyright music in public on your premises, whether it is through a radio, television, CD player, video recorder or any other mechanical device, or if it is played live. See the Appendix for contact numbers and websites.

Wine list

Another decision to be made relates to the wine list if you have a licence. In a small property, you will not sell huge amounts of wine. However, for discerning guests who enjoy a bottle of wine, it is nice to have a reasonable selection.

If you select wines which are always available from your local supplier or cash and carry, then you do not need to pay to carry a large stock. If you work on overdraft, it is better to have the money in the bank than on the wine shelves! Remember, however, that there is usually a reduction for buying full cases (six bottles nowadays) rather than odd bottles.

The sections of a wine list are simple. You need a white section, a rosé section and a red section, usually listed in that order.

How far you want to go is really up to the requirements of your guests, although you might want to put on a really good wine in each category, alongside the popular ones that are generally ordered by guests. It is nice to have Croze Hermitage and Premier Cru Chablis, but not to carry them in stock for years if they do not sell.

A simple example might be that you have as white wines, a Pinot Grigio, a Chardonnay, perhaps a German wine which is more fruity and less dry to suit the palate of the non-dry wine drinkers, and then if you want, a more expensive wine.

For the rosé wines, two would suffice with a Rosé de Provence as the ordinary one and an Anjou as the better one.

For the reds, a Valpollicella, a Côte du Rhône, maybe a Beaujolais, and then something special to offer as better type of wine.

I have suggested these wines simply because they are generally fairly big sellers at a reasonable cost, which means you can charge a fair rate and make a reasonable gross profit. In writing the list, take some information from the label and give the guests a thumbnail sketch of the attributes of the wine.

The selections you make should relate to the tastes and requirements of your guests, otherwise you will not sell any wine. In addition to the bottle list, it is wise to offer wine by the glass. Be sure to tell the guests the wine glass size so they can judge if the price is acceptable. Remember that wines in the bottle deteriorate when exposed to the air and so it might be preferable to use wine boxes. These last better since the wine is packed in a vacuum which crumples up as the wine goes out. You can now also buy glass-sized bottles with a good range of varieties with which your guests might be familiar.

Although I have only given you an example of a simple wine list, you may feel that you wish to make wine a feature and have more spectacular ones on display in part of your dining room area. A more extensive wine list might be of more interest to your particular guests. In that case, go for it, but remember the problem of carrying a large stock and also the security aspect of open wine racks in the dining area.

Pricing is your decision and again, it depends what price is acceptable to your guests. There is no point in having a wine which is priced to give you a £15.00 gross profit if you never sell any. Better to have a £6.00 or £7.00 gross profit and sell a couple every night. If the bottle cost you £3.00 and you sell it for £10.00, then your gross profit is £7.00. Trial and error is the key and be flexible when you start up and see what your customers think of your choices and your prices.

There is a pricing policy which is sometimes used which you may wish to consider. This policy sets a cash level of gross profit for each wine offered and which is applied to the purchase price. For example, if I buy a bottle of Valpollicella for £3.50 and I have decided that the gross profit I want to achieve on all bottled wines is £6.00, then I would sell the wine for £9.50. The benefit of this to the guest is that if you buy the Cordon Rouge (Champagne) for £12.00, then they get the benefit of real value for money when you sell it for £18.00.

Wine service

Wine service is not complex and one suggestion I would make is to use a bottle opener that you can handle. The 'waiter's friend' is a trusted bottle opener for the professionals, however, many people find it difficult to handle. Use the one you are comfortable with and follow the standard rules, namely:

◆ Present the ordered bottle to the host for confirmation that it is the correct bottle. Be sure to show the label.

◆ Open the bottle in view of the guest.

◆ Offer the host the opportunity to taste the wine. Pour a small amount in the glass for the host to taste. Obtain the go ahead to pour.

◆ Serve ladies first, then the gentlemen, then fill the host's glass.

◆ Keep white and rosé wine chilled, and red wine at room temperature.

◆ Top up as required.

Selling wine and drinks

In a small property, sales techniques should not be cut-throat to the point that guests feel uncomfortable and put upon. On the other hand, they may feel embarrassed to ask for an alcoholic drink, so break the ice and give information about what you have available. Don't push bottle sales if you feel they might only want a glass of wine.

Print little cards of wine specials which might relate to a particular menu item and let the guests make the decision rather than feeling they are being pushed in to it.

When coffee has been served, give the offer of a liqueur or a malt whisky, but do not put excess pressure on. If they feel that the pressure has been excessive, they may not come back for dinner.

> **Keep your sales pitch at the information level and learn on day one what the guest likes and follow this through for the rest of their stay.**

Hygiene

When you are in the business of food service, you have a responsibility to make sure that the food you sell is safe to eat and that your premises are conducive to the hygienic and safe preparation of food. You have available to you the benefit of the services of the local

Environmental Health Officer (EHO) and you should contact this office to obtain useful advice on practices and on aspects relating to your property to ensure the safety of your guests, staff and yourselves. An excellent contact on the internet is www.food.gov.uk/cleanup and it is strongly recommended that this site is visited.

If you do not have experience in the industry, it is recommended that you take a course on hygiene, and your local college will probably offer such a course. The EHO will be able to give you information about such courses also.

Food poisoning, or food-borne illness as it is better known nowadays, occurs for many reasons and some of the most commonly mentioned causes are the following:

1. Failure to properly refrigerate foods.

2. Failure to bring cold foods to hot as quickly as possible or hot foods to cold as quickly as possible.

3. Poor personal hygiene practices of food handlers.

4. Foods prepared too far in advance of use.

5. Contaminated raw foods incorporated into foods which receive no further cooking.

6. Foods that are allowed to remain at temperatures which will allow bacteria to incubate.

7. Failure to reheat cooked foods to temperatures that kill bacteria.

8. Cross-contamination of cooked foods with raw items, either through faulty storage, poorly cleaned equipment or food handlers who mishandle foods.

Your responsibility, then, is to eliminate these problem areas. This requires an understanding of some key factors related to bacterial growth and the problem of cross-contamination. While this section of this book is not intended to give an all-inclusive approach to issues of hygiene in a small hotel environment, I believe an understanding of these factors may be helpful before the inexperienced operator attends a hygiene course.

Causes of food poisoning

There are essentially two causes of food poisoning.

The first is chemical poisoning caused by chemicals and pesticides, and there are some precautions which can be taken to avoid this problem. The first is to learn something about the sources of the foods you buy and be sure that your suppliers are reputable and dependable. Inspect their premises if you are unsure. As far as chemical sprays and insecticides are concerned, be sure to wash all fruits and vegetables before use. Keep all chemicals and items like insecticides and poison for vermin away from foods and in a separate storage area.

The second is germs which are harmful to humans. Germs are small living organisms, most, but not all, of which are dangerous. The dangerous ones cause disease and illness if they are allowed to multiply and spread to humans through food or any other contact.

Germs needs some special conditions to grow. They need a comfortable temperature, food, moisture, and time at the right temperature, to multiply.

The food that most bacteria like, tend to be the foods that humans like. They like non-acid, high protein foods like meats, fish, poultry, milk and eggs. They also like cream, and foods which contain dairy products and eggs and any combination of the above.

They need moisture in order to be able to multiply. Drying or freezing removes moisture. However the germs are not killed. They merely lie dormant until such time as the food is reconstituted or thawed.

Germs require a comfortable temperature to multiply and the danger zone for optimum bacterial growth is 45 to 140 degrees Fahrenheit (7 to 60 degrees Celsius). Keeping foods out of this temperature range is the aim, and foods should be heated through it or cooled quickly through the range. This means that putting a container of soup in a bain-marie at 4.00p.m. to heat up for dinner at 7.00p.m. is highly dangerous. The soup should be placed in a pot on the stove at 6.45p.m. and quickly brought to the boil prior to service. If service continues until 7.30p.m., the soup should be allowed to simmer, thereby retaining a heat above the danger area.

Similarly, soups or stocks, which are made in advance, should be cooled as quickly as possible through the range by using an ice bath into which the soup pot is placed. When cool, the soup should be placed in the refrigerator. This should not occur while still hot, as it would raise the temperature in the refrigerator and compromise all the other items in it.

In optimum conditions, bacteria multiply every 20 minutes, so food items left in the kitchen where moisture and the right temperature exist, are exposed to hazardous conditions.

It can be seen that a kitchen which is dirty with food particles and is warm and moist, will over a very short time enable bacterial growth.

Avoiding cross-contamination

As we have seen, there are a number of ways in which cross-contamination can occur and all can be avoided relatively easily. Cross-contamination generally occurs when already cooked foods are contaminated by raw foods.

A common example of this happening would be to dissect a chicken on a chopping board and then, use the same board to slice cold roast beef for salads. Bacteria from the chicken contaminates the salad beef with the likely result of causing food-borne illness for the guests who eat the salad.

The solution to this problem is to have colour-coded boards for different uses and ensure that the boards are only used for the correct purpose. In addition, the need for cleaning down the area with soap and water between uses is paramount.

Another simple, yet effective method of avoiding cross-contamination is good storage in the refrigerator. Keep all items in containers with covered lids and, as an extra precaution, make sure that cooked items are stored above raw items, so that any dripping that might take place will not affect the cooked foods.

Hygiene training will involve considerably more than this. However, this is key information which should help an operator to avoid food contamination.

Self inspection

The local EHO will inspect your premises at some point. However, it is a good practice for you to put on your health inspector hat yourself and critically examine your own property from time to time.

Consider the following areas:

◆ personal hygiene of all food-handlers

◆ food storage areas such as stores, refrigerators, and freezers

◆ food-handling practices, i.e prevention of cross-contamination and care in eliminating optimum conditions for bacterial growth as previously mentioned

◆ cleanliness of food-handling areas and equipment

◆ cleanliness of dishwashing and dish storage areas

- ◆ cleanliness of staff and your toilets and signs for 'Now Wash Your Hands'

- ◆ cleanliness of equipment storage areas

- ◆ location and orderliness of rubbish disposal areas.

Be prepared to put on your white coat and get a torch and pull out equipment, look behind cupboards, in the freezer and in the refrigerator and generally be critical in order to find any potential problems. Having identified problems, take steps to eliminate them and change routines so they do not happen again.

Reporting food-borne illness

While your instincts might steer you away from reporting the possibility of food-borne illness, in reality it is most important to report it to your local EHO in order that an investigation can take place.

If a guest or staff member has been taken ill, make the call and do not throw away any remaining food that was served. Make notes of the events of the day and most particularly what each guest or staff member ate. List all foods served to each guest since one guest might have become ill and not another, after eating the same food. List where the food was purchased and wait to see the result of the investigation. It might have nothing to do with your premises or it might have to do with food purchased from a particular supplier. You need to find out so do not hide anything.

Summary

This aim of this extensive chapter has been to present the reader with some ideas on the complexity of the food and beverage side of a small hotel. I have also aimed to show that, while it is an area which is physically demanding, if it is planned and set up well, it is very rewarding and more importantly, it is fun! In addition, it has shown the need for control of the perishable products used in food and beverage as well as some suggestions on the purchasing of products and equipment. Most importantly, it has introduced the reader to aspects of hygiene, which is a great responsibility for anyone involved in the sale of food.

The following are the action steps for Chapter 6:

◆ Draft your breakfast menu.

◆ Bearing your level of ability in mind, draft your dinner menus.

◆ If you offer lunch, draft lunch menu.

◆ Decide on portion sizes.

◆ Develop recipes.

◆ Develop purchase specifications.

◆ Cost out dishes.

◆ Calculate food cost percentage.

◆ Calculate bar and wine cost percentage.

◆ Prepare an equipment list (based on the existing inventory).

◆ Decide on style of food service.

◆ Plan your wine list.

◆ Develop a plan for good hygienic practice.

CHAPTER SEVEN

Housekeeping Issues

Isn't it strange that as guests in hotels, we are prepared to sleep in a bed that other people slept in the previous night, and use a bath or shower as well as the toilet that others used just that morning. We are only prepared to accept this without thinking about it, however, if the room is in pristine condition and shows no signs of any previous occupancy. No hairs in the bath, no crushed duvet cover, no debris on the carpet and no litter in the bin.

We have spoken in Chapter 4 about 'getting it right the first time' and this is what we have to do when preparing the room. In fact, we have to get it right every time.

The role of the small hotel operator in terms of the 'housekeeping department' is the same as that for any size of hotel. They must ensure the cleanliness of all areas and the effective maintenance of the whole operation and also create and maintain the anticipated aesthetic appeal of the property.

Having said that, in a very small property, this department uses the same personnel as the other departments, namely the owners, and so they must plan their work schedules to give as much importance to this area of operation as any other. They are all vital: the work involved just takes place at a different time.

You may or may not have any professional experience in this area, although if you have followed some of my earlier suggestions, you might have decided to gain some experience in a hotel. If you do this, do not ignore this area as it is as important as any other, and some good information and methods of operation will be obtained.

If you have professional experience, consider what your guest expectations are, as well as your current staffing arrangements, and work out how you will achieve the former with the latter.

First impressions

You only get one chance to make a good first impression!

Let me say again, that this frequently used cliché is a very real statement of fact in our industry. While clearly, the very first impression is achieved when you answer the telephone, or write a letter and send a brochure in response to an inquiry, the real first impression is when the guests ring the bell and you welcome them into your property.

Many things come into play then, including eye contact, friendliness, and help with luggage, but the guest is also taking in the visual aspects of their entrance to the property, including neatness, cleanliness, decor, lightness and brightness, and even smell. These are the areas to consider when addressing the first impression issue.

The next step is to take the guests to their room and the same issues apply, although now, this is to become their territory and they are more diligent in making their assessment. Mrs Guest will make a beeline for the bathroom to check that it meets her expectations. Mr Guest will sit on the bed to check that the mattress is in good condition and will be itching for you to leave so he can make sure the TV is working.

> **Housekeeping is so important that it has to be carried out meticulously every time and the way to be sure of this is to have a tried and tested routine which is repeated in every room, every day and which results in a spotless and acceptable room.**

Bedroom cleaning routines

The first step for the room cleaner before setting foot in the room is to assemble all the items needed. Two types of cleaning may take place: the first would be for a check-out room and the second for a room clean when the guests are still in-house.

Assembling the necessary equipment is best done on some kind of trolley. This does not need to be the size of a regular hotel trolley but can be a smaller version which will hold sufficient supplies for the smaller number of rooms you have. It is also possible to have such a trolley which can be taken up stairs and which adapts to this. The trolley should have a space for dirty linen and for rubbish from the rooms.

Alternatively, if your property is on one floor, have a housekeeping room or cupboard if possible, in a central position to all the rooms, thereby eliminating the need for a trolley.

Two types of supplies are needed, replacement supplies and cleaning supplies, as shown in Figure 7.1.

Replacement supplies	Cleaning supplies
Sheets	Rubber gloves
Pillowslips	Cleaning cloths
Mattress pads	Polishing cloths
Towels	All purpose cleaner
Wash cloths	Glass cleaner
Bathmats	Toilet cleaner
Glasses	Mildew remover
Amenities (shampoo, soaps, cotton buds, nail files etc)	
Soap	
Ashtrays/matches (if applicable)	

Figure 7.1. Bedroom cleaning supplies.

Having assembled the supplies, go to the room and follow this procedure:

1. Turn on the lights so you can see well and to check that all light bulbs are working.

2. Open the windows to air the room and look around to assess the condition of the room.

3. Remove dirty ashtrays and water glasses and replace with clean ones. Collect up any rubbish and take it and the rubbish bin to the trolley. If you use bin liners, replace the liner in the bin.

4. Remove sheets, pillowslips and duvet covers from the bed. You may wish to take them directly to the washer to get the laundry going as early as possible.

5. Make the bed. No special instructions here other than a guest expectation that the bed is comfortable to be in and that the sheets etc. will stay on and that they look clean, smell fresh and show signs of pressing. In the case of the make-up room, the sheets will be checked and if in good order, the bed will be remade. Change of sheets is usual every second or third day for long-stay guests.

6. Dust the room. Begin in one spot and work around the room until you reach where you started. Dust from high to low. If using a dusting spray, spray it onto the dusting cloth and not directly onto the surfaces as it can stain. The items to be dusted should include

pictures, door tops, mirror tops, headboards, bedside tables, telephone, TV, chairs, shelves, doorknobs, heaters, fans.

7. Clean mirrors and picture with a glass-cleaning agent.

8. The last task is to vacuum the room and this should be done after the bathroom is cleaned. Before starting with the vacuum, look under the edge of the beds and furniture and pull out any pieces of fluff or rubbish that is visible. Vacuum all surface areas making sure everything is picked up and make vacuum cleaner lines towards the door so that it is obvious to the arriving guest that the room has indeed been vacuumed. Moving heavy items, with some assistance, and vacuuming this area, can be an occasional duty, perhaps once a month.

9. The very last thing is a final check. This is done by starting at one point in the room and carefully looking at all aspects of the room to see if anything has not been done. If you have air fresheners, make sure you can smell them and, if not, check if they need to be replaced. Switch off the light.

Bath/shower/toilet cleaning routines

There is a logical sequence to cleaning a bath or shower room. However, one important part of the process should always be to work from top to bottom. The sequence recommended is to clean the shower area, then the sink and the vanity, the toilet, the walls and the fixtures and then the floor. If there is a bath, this should be cleaned after the walls or tiles above it.

1. Clean the shower area from the top to the bottom using an all-purpose cleaner, looking out for hairs stuck to the wall or in the grout of the tiles. Look out for the start of mould build up and the possibility of rust marks and mildew. Mildew remover spray should be used at the first sign of mildew. Use a toothbrush for this kind of cleaning which requires fine detailed work. Check all tracks and corners where moisture collects. Check the drain and the shower curtain for hair. Where the shower is of enclosed glass, dry, clean and polish the glass.

2. With all-purpose cleaner, clean the sink and the vanity. Again, check for hairs. Remove all evidence of toothpaste from the shelf. Rinse, dry and polish any chrome fittings. Polish the mirror using glass cleaner.

3. Flush the toilet and apply a bacterial bathroom cleaner around the bowl and under the lip. Allow it to stand for some time if possible. If you have a septic tank, make sure it is an appropriate cleaner. Scrub the toilet with the brush around the inside and under the lip. Finally, flush the toilet again. Clean the top of the seat with a damp cloth and cleaner and dry it with a dry cloth. Now wipe down the sides of the toilet.

4. Clean the toilet brush and empty and dry the toilet brush container.

5. Stock the bath or shower room with the requisite amounts of towels, face cloths and any amenities that need replenishing.

6. Inspect the walls for any necessary spot cleaning.

7. Starting at the furthest away point, clean the floor using an all-purpose cleaner in water, and then dry in the same way. Check the skirting board at this time.

8. Wipe down bathroom door including the door handles and the top of the door.

9. Replace pedestal/bathmat.

Some hotels give guests the option of having their towels changed by having a notice in the bathroom which requests that towels to be changed, be placed in the shower or the bath. This is suggested for environmental reasons relating to water and electricity consumption and pollution. Guests generally seem to be happy to go along with this. We overrule the policy sometimes if we feel the towels need to be changed and the change has not been requested. Such notices can be obtained from your local tourist authority.

Cleaning routines for public areas

Entrance area

Remember that part of the first impression is what guests see when they walk in the door.

The front desk or arrival hallway area should be warm, welcoming, clean and tidy, and should have a fresh smell. Since this area is likely to be used when guests are leaving and when guests are arriving, it should probably receive attention last thing at night, ready for departures in the morning and again after departures. This will leave it spick and span, ready for arrivals.

This should consist of tidying the area, wiping down and polishing any furniture that needs polishing, and dusting lights and ornaments and even flowers if they are artificial. Fresh flower arrangements should be checked for decay and for the water, which may develop a smell if not changed regularly. Emptying rubbish bins and vacuuming the carpet finishes the entrance area.

Consider also a routine for cleaning windows and any glass doors. You may decide that this should be carried out by a window cleaner and if so, be sure to check the quality of work carried out before making payment.

If your local tourist brochures are in this area, straighten and tidy them routinely every morning or even late evening.

Corridors and hallways

The most important part of keeping this area in good order is vacuuming the carpet. If there is furniture in this area, it should be dusted and occasionally polished. You may find that the carpet gets dirty frequently and it may be worth having a mechanical carpet sweeper just to quickly sweep the carpet in the dirty area without the need for getting out the vacuum. I find that I use this many times during the day to keep the carpet always looking fresh and clean.

Public rooms

Areas such as the lounge, the dining room and the bar will need constant attention and should be tidied after every period of use. In the lounge, books and magazines should be tidied last thing in the evening, and furniture put back in place. In the evening, you may not wish to use the vacuum because of the noise, so the carpet sweeper can be used to freshen and clean the carpet. Vacuuming is likely to take place in the morning, after guests have gone out for the day when the noise factor of vacuuming in not important.

There should be a routine for dusting and polishing and while polishing does not need to be done every day, dusting should be a daily routine.

It is worth pointing out that the chances are that one or other of the partners will tend to work in certain areas of the property exclusively. My domain, if you like, is the dining room/lounge and bar, and cleanliness of this area is checked by routine inspections by my wife, who is able to spot things that I have missed, and so we try to keep things in best possible condition by inspecting each other's areas.

Carpets

Carpets have many purposes in a guesthouse or hotel and they offer many benefits. They are, however, costly if you decide to purchase or replace with high quality carpeting so they should be cared for on a routine basis to prolong the life. It is recommended that a high quality purchase will pay off, in that the life of the carpet will be much longer than a less expensive product.

Carpets reduce noise and limit echo effect due to the absorption of sound. They keep floors and rooms warmer and they prevent slipping. Sometimes it seems a shame to cover wooden floors, but the above are good reasons for doing so.

The higher quality, more durable carpets have dense fibres and they tend to be the better buy, albeit more expensive. Another advantage is that because of their density, they keep dirt and stains on the top and are therefore easier to clean.

Each day, when room cleaning takes place, the carpets should be inspected for spots and spills and they should be dealt with as soon as possible. Spot removers are generally obtainable, even from your local supermarket. Follow the instructions and vacuum the carpet after cleaning has taken place. To avoid carpets getting muddy and dirty, a preventive approach is useful in making sure that guests have what they need to clean shoes as they enter the property. Have shoe scrapers situated at the entrance and have mats on carpets at entrance doors. This should help to remove dirt which otherwise would be walked throughout the property.

During food service, I place a mat on the hallway floor outside the kitchen to avoid wear and tear as I step out and turn my foot to change direction. This I hope will save wearing in one spot, which might mean the entire hallway carpet has to be replaced earlier than it need be. It also prevents crumbs, perhaps grease, etc. from the kitchen being trodden into the carpet. This not only looks bad but also may leave a permanent stain.

The carpet should be shampooed at least once a year in a seasonal property and twice in a property that has greater activity. Some manufacturers recommend dry powder cleaning, which absorbs oily dirt which can then be removed by vacuuming. Follow the manufacturer's instructions for carpet cleaning.

You should plan for carpet replacement. It is a high cost item and it might be wise to take the time to inspect all carpets and give them your own quality rating and then prioritise replacement accordingly over a number of years. In Chapter 4, in the section regarding the quality assurance process, I suggested looking at the fine detail of your quality assessment process. The link I suggested through www.scotexchange/

businessdevelopment, then Quality Assurance, then Guesthouses, then Grading, then Bedrooms, then 'floorings', gives good details of the type of floorings which attract the highest assessment and how they should be kept. This is an example of using your quality assurance scheme to help you to plan strategically and make good decisions.

Linen stock

Large hotels will tend to work with a par of five for linen. This means that for each item, e.g. a sheet for a single bed in room three, there should be five on the property. One on the bed; one in the linen cupboard, just in from the laundry; one dirty going to be washed; one replacement stock and one for emergencies. By the way, purists will tell you that linen should rest for 24 hours between washing and reuse in order to lengthen the life of the item. We find, however, that we can work very comfortably with a par of three, where we have one on the bed, one being washed and one in the linen cupboard. I imagine that some properties even work with less that this. Having an in-house laundry makes this possible for us.

We have found that with linen, as with many things, it pays to purchase best quality, particularly if you have a low stock, since it means that each item is washed more often than if you had a larger stock.

Storage of linen should be in a dry place with reduced humidity and with good ventilation. Shelves should be smooth and clean, ideally with a covering or gloss painted. Some properties use bars of their favourite smelling soap randomly placed between items to give a pleasant smell to the linen.

Laundry issues

To launder in-house or not, that is the question. There are pros and cons. However, the most important factor is the cost of laundering externally, as well as the problem of delivery, and possibly the need for an increased stock. We made the decision to launder ourselves and while this gives us more work, there is no doubt that it reduces our costs, and we believe it is likely to lengthen the life of our linen. We look after it and inspect it on a daily basis.

At present we use two domestic washers and two domestic dryers, although we hang laundry out to dry as much as possible. We finish towels in the dryer to give a fluffy finish. We have an industrial rotary iron, which is very easy to use and produces a professional result. When any of the washers and driers stop working, we will replace it with a commercial unit or, at least, one of the larger American top loading washers and a bigger drier which would hold three times the volume and take less time.

The easiest bed linen to work with is a combination of cotton and polyester. This is more crease resistant and is therefore easy and quick to launder and press. The finished product looks fresh and professional, particularly when well pressed.

When replacing, as with most items which have heavy usage, it is a false economy to purchase inexpensive linens and it is recommended that best brand names and good quality products are purchased. The purchase price is likely to be higher, but wear and tear will be reduced and the items will last for longer.

Bathroom amenities and guest expectations

The guest supplies or amenities that you have as 'free' items in the guest room and bathroom will depend on the prices charged for the room. Clearly big hotels that charge high rates and have the luxury of bulk purchasing and leverage with suppliers will be able to offer more and will also have reduced unit costs due to purchase volume.

The small hotelier has to decide what the guests might expect and try to meet this expectation and possibly exceed it. Our guesthouse has 'middle-of-the-road' prices but we decided to have our guest amenities at a good level in order to create a 'wow' factor with out guests. We have not gone totally overboard, but generally our guests comment that they are pleasantly surprised with what they find in the bathroom and the room. Our list is as follows:

◆ shampoo and shower gel
◆ liquid hand-wash soap. For environmental reasons, we use refillable containers of shampoo and soap and we find this to be acceptable to guests particularly for the same reasons
◆ individual wrapped guest soap as an alternative to liquid soap
◆ cotton buds
◆ cotton wool cleansing pads

- nail file
- sewing kit
- tissues in bathroom and bedroom
- in addition to bath towels, towelling bath mat and hand towels, we also offer washcloths, which many hotels do not. We do not offer bath sheets due to the difficulty in washing and drying them.

> **With repeat guests or long-stay guests, you may wish to consider special 'gifts' such as hand lotion which you may even wish to gift wrap.**

In purchasing there is always the dilemma of holding stock on the shelves rather than money in the bank, but it is clear that when you purchase in bulk, the unit cost is cheaper. Next time you visit the cash and carry, compare unit prices for a small quantity and large quantities of the same product. In addition, we buy bulk soap, shampoo and tissues. You have to make the decision on how many of each item you need. Remember that after your first year, if you keep records, you will have good statistics on usage, therefore you will know how many of each item to purchase for a certain given period of time.

Cleaning equipment and products

In order to make a good job of the housekeeping aspect of your business, it is necessary to have the right equipment and to use the right chemicals and commercial products for the particular task to be carried out. There are many products for sale which can be bought through the local cash and carry, or even through the local supermarket.

The equipment needed will be as you might expect, including:

- brush
- brush and dustpan
- toothbrush (for grouting etc.)
- dust mop
- wet mop and bucket
- spray bottles

- rubber gloves
- rags, polishing and cleaning cloths
- carpet sweeper
- vacuum – it may be an idea to have one for each floor if you have multiple floors
- carpet shampoo machine.

As mentioned, the chemicals and products required for the various tasks can be easily purchased and you should study the properties of each and consider the result in relation to the cost before making a decision on what you will use. Have a period when you test-use different products to see which suits you best of all and then make your decision.

Special cleaning problems

In addition to the normal cleaning process which you will carry out using the above equipment and the products you have chosen, from time to time you will need to carry out occasional special cleaning. Particular problems will crop up that require special care and attention. Handling this aspect of the business may well save your linen or other assets of the business, so it is worth dealing with such problems in an effective way.

Figure 7.2 shows some of the problems that occasionally crop up and which need special treatment. In addition to these remedies, there are some specialist cleaning materials, which can be purchased, for example for the removal of blood. It is recommended that if you are going to use them, that you try them out on samples of your linen to see what works best on that particular material. Many of these products can now be purchased in your local supermarket.

Occasional and special cleaning

The cleaning you carry out on a daily basis will keep the rooms in good condition and will keep the appearance of the hotel/guesthouse at an ideal level for a period of time.

From time to time, however, it will be necessary to carry out a special cleaning, similar to a domestic spring-cleaning, which you would carry out at home. If your business is seasonal then this can best be done in the off-season, ideally before the start of the

Problem	Action	Product
Nail polish	Remove immediately with a dry cloth, taking care not to spread the stain.	Remove with rubbing alcohol and rinse off with water.
Urine, blood	Wash stained area as soon as possible with soapy water and bleach. Rinse.	Strong soapy solution Chlorinated bleach
Paint, tar, shoe scuffmarks, oil	Rub off as much as possible then clean with turpentine or turpentine substitute. Rinse thoroughly with water.	Turpentine or substitute
Ballpoint ink marks	Remove as soon as possible by rubbing with a cloth and rubbing alcohol.	Rubbing alcohol
Pencil or crayon	Scrape off any crayon you can remove with a knife. Not a cutting motion. Erase pencil marks using a normal eraser. Remove remaining stains with rubbing alcohol.	Rubbing alcohol Pencil eraser
Chewing gum	Wipe off as much as possible with a cloth wrapped round an ice cube. Rub lightly with rubbing alcohol.	Ice Rubbing alcohol
Mustard	Wash out in soapy water.	Soap
Tea	Wash out with strong detergent in warm water.	Strong detergent
Lipstick	Wash out with strong detergent in warm water.	Strong detergent

Figure 7.2 Dealing with stains.

season, so that the property is spotlessly clean and fresh for the guests arriving in the new season. Removal of as much furniture as possible before carrying out such a cleaning is recommended.

The aim of this special cleaning is to:

◆ dust difficult-to-reach areas
◆ clean the blades of fans
◆ clean bathroom filters on extracts
◆ move furniture for all-round vacuuming
◆ shampoo carpets
◆ wiping down walls and touch up paint if necessary
◆ wash curtains and net screens
◆ wash Venetian blinds
◆ vacuum mattresses.

If the property does not close on a seasonal basis, such a cleaning is more complex and sometimes, due to pressure of business, it is easy to avoid doing it since if the rooms are let, the money continues to roll in. Beware of this and be sure to allocate a day or two for each room on at least an annual basis to carry out the cleaning. It may be necessary to have extra staff to do this cleaning, and clearly, the quicker it is done, the quicker the room is bringing in revenue again. Certainly, this type of cleaning should be planned when the hotel/guesthouse is likely to have its lowest occupancy period in order to minimise the loss of revenue. If any maintenance tasks need to be carried out, then this is the time to have these jobs done as well.

Turndown service

The concept of the turndown service is one that seems to be dying out other than in the more expensive hotels. We have found that the quality advisors of the organisations we are affiliated to seem to like the idea, although since we use duvets, it seems like something of an overkill to offer the service. In addition, if you are running a small property as a two-person team and serving dinners, finding the time for such as service would be difficult. We do not do it, but this is something for you to consider as an extra service to your guests.

Décor

Clearly, the décor will be the way you stamp your personality on the property and you will no doubt take into account the area and local heritage in selecting the décor and the style of your rooms. Remember that you are trying to produce a product that will be acceptable to your particular target market and the style they are likely to want should be what is produced.

One small issue that I believe is important, is that rooms should be homely yet standardised and professional, while meeting all the needs of the guests. They should not be titillated with bits and pieces of your personal items so that the guests feel they are in your personal room. This will make them feel uncomfortable. Pictures of granny with the kids will not cut it! The rooms should not be bland, but should have character, possibly reflecting the local area, but not be a museum of your family collectables and heirlooms.

Some properties create character with local artefacts or artwork in public areas, and this is acceptable since they can become talking points for the guests.

Summary

The idea that you only get one chance to make a good first impression is very relevant to the housekeeping area. The guest's first impression of the inside of the property and then the guest room if positive, sets the scene for a comfortable and enjoyable stay. Our product is the room we sell and it must be good. Routines to achieve this have been presented in terms of the cleaning of public areas, bedrooms and bathrooms, both routinely and for occasional deep cleaning. In addition, the level of linen stock and the use of a 'home' laundry have been discussed. Decisions have to be made regarding what amenities are offered and also what equipment is required to complete the housekeeping operation.

The following are the action steps for Chapter 7:

◆ Gain relevant experience if you currently have none in this area.

◆ Draft a bedroom cleaning performance standard.

◆ Plan for purchase of cleaning and replacement supplies.

◆ Draft a bathroom cleaning performance standard.

◆ Draft a public areas cleaning performance standard.

◆ Take inventory of existing linen and plan a linen stock par.

◆ Take decisions regarding laundry policy and, if required, plan for an effective and efficient in-house laundry.

◆ Make a decision on guest amenities.

◆ Ensure good supplies of cleaning equipment and products.

◆ Make an assessment of carpeting needs for the future.

◆ When necessary, plan 'special cleaning' routines.

CHAPTER EIGHT

Marketing and Advertising

What is marketing?

Marketing really has to do with:

- creating something which potential customers want
- offering it in a place which is convenient and attractive to the customers
- offering it at a price which is reasonable and fair, which offers the customers value for money and is competitive
- letting potential customers know about the product or service through the many forms of communication available to you.

Now, as mentioned previously it is to be hoped that your 'product' is something that the guests want and this is the reason you bought the guesthouse. It is also to be hoped that you have purchased your guesthouse or hotel in a location which is convenient and attractive to potential guests. Having said this we have not investigated how to describe this customer who is likely to want what you offer, where you offer it and at the price you offer it. It is important to know as much as you can about your potential guests.

If the property was up and running before you bought it, you have almost certainly discussed this with the previous owners. At this point you should have learned from them:

- the age group of your customers
- their external interests that cause them to stay in this guesthouse/hotel
- the geographical area from which they come
- what makes the guesthouse important to them
- their willingness to pay for what you offer
- their average length of stay.

Confirmation of these facts is important and this is yet another arm of marketing, which is known as market research. It sounds formal, but at this stage, it has to do with talking to and listening to your customers.

When you check guests in and ask them to register, you can ask a few additional questions on the form, which will give you added information. We ask how they heard of our guesthouse. The answer to this question indicates the advertisement which is working best for us. Because we have done this, we have become very clear about which advertising is the best. We are also pleased to find that many of our guests come from recommendations or referrals from guests who have stayed with us previously.

Recommendations and referrals

Since this has proven to be good for our business, let us investigate it a little bit further. Once you have a base of good, repeat customers, who are prepared to talk about you to their friends and colleagues, you must do all you can to hold on to them and look after them. Bear in mind that the best and cheapest form of advertising is word of mouth.

Making contact with known guests from time to time just keeps your name in their thoughts. Consider also that in our industry, our ultimate product is memories. By making contact, the memory of your property, your area, your hospitality, their relaxation and hopefully, a warm feeling, is rekindled. We make contact with our repeat guests in three ways.

Firstly, we send all guests a Christmas card and for the guests who are repeats or who we feel have become friends, we take time to write a few lines as you would to any other friend. If there is any special event that happened during the holiday with us, we mention this to personalise the card. For example, we had a lady staying with us who was on a walking holiday, and one day she slipped and broke her ankle. Firstly, at the time, we went out of our way to assist her and offer meals at special times, etc., but secondly, we talked about it in the Christmas card and just wished her well. Another trick is to buy your Christmas cards in the sales in January and, as each guest checks out throughout the year, write their Christmas card. This also saves a major chore in December! One way to enable you to personalise such cards is to create a 'guest history' which can be a database in the computer or individual cards on which you write any little bits and pieces to help you remember the guests. This was mentioned in more detail in Chapter 5.

Occasionally, as time permits, we buy some local scene postcards and just drop a personal card to guests that we see quite often. While we do this because we see them as friends, it also helps to stimulate their interest again in the area and maybe have them consider another vacation with us. It might also be that this will cause them to talk with friends and colleagues and a new connection might be made.

Thirdly, this year, we decided on a 'loyalty' concept and sent a direct mail offer to many repeat guests for two-day and three-day dinner, bed and breakfast specials in our 'shoulder season' when the business was beginning to slacken off. This was very successful in that we stayed busy until the end of the season, we gave our regulars an excellent, value for money special and we finished off the season by seeing lots of our old friends.

Our next plan is to take this a stage further and when we know that a current guest has referred new guests, we will offer the referrer a ten per cent discount on their next stay as a reward. We will be proactive and send existing guests two ten per cent off vouchers, one which they can use and one which they can pass on to a friend. If you do this, you may wish to restrict the ten per cent to the accommodation only and not to food or drinks.

> **In short, repeats and referrals can be your core market and you must show them recognition and look after them the best way you can.**

Geographically targeted marketing

The guest registration card will give you information on where your guests come from, and if you wish to take the time to analyse this, it will be very useful to you.

We find that of the English guests, the majority are from Yorkshire, Lancashire, Staffordshire and Birmingham, so in the case that we decide to do any 'impulse' or single-shot advertising, then we can target particular areas. In listening to guests during service and general chatting, we have found that many make an overnight stop on their way to us, at guesthouses in a particular small town at about the halfway point.

This year, we are sending copies of our brochures to these guesthouses in the hope that they will be seen by other guests who may wish to book ahead for their next night or hopefully longer. Similarly, as a service to our guests, we hold many brochures of other guesthouses so that we can help guests find comparable accommodation as they continue their vacation. They are always happy to have recommendations of similar type of properties. It is generally a good idea to make a visit if you can, to be able to recommend, but failing this, listen to your guests talking about their experiences in other guesthouses and make notes.

As a service to your guests, build a group of like unofficial 'partners', that you can recommend and who are far enough away not to be competition.

Pricing

Value for money is a most important factor for guests and you must bear this in mind when setting the price.

There is a formula which has been used in the hotel industry for a number of years, called the Hubbart formula, which takes into consideration operating costs, capital costs and a target profit to calculate a selling price. It sounds good, but what if the price you come up with in your small property is out of line with the price your guests want to pay, as well as the price your competitors are offering? While it might be of interest to work this out, you need to establish what is acceptable to your guests and what will be competitive.

Obviously, if you are taking over an operating business, prices already exist and indeed, you may be locked into them due to advertising that has already been done. If you are opening a new business, then clearly a survey of the local competition is necessary in order to come up with a charge which corresponds to the 'going rate' locally. The resultant decision on pricing should be built into the accounts in the business plan.

Your property may have some added advantages which enable you to make a higher charge. Perhaps the competition is not en-suite but you are. Perhaps your décor, complete with fresh flowers, means that you can charge more. Perhaps the four-poster bed in your most elegant room means that you charge a bit more. Sometimes, the room with the best view will command a better price than the room which overlooks the car park. In addition, in a seasonal establishment, perhaps the beginning of the season will have lower charges than the high season, i.e. March, April and October, November may have a lower price structure than the summer months. Another aspect of pricing might relate to reduced rates for longer stays. We have a rate for up to two nights, a different rate from three to six nights inclusive and then an even better rate for seven or more nights. We also offer an inclusive dinner, bed and breakfast rate for seven nights, which is a considerable advantage over seven nights bed and breakfast rate with dinner added on a daily basis.

When I was a young man in this business, a very sage old hotel manager told me that a room is like fresh cream. If you don't use it today, it cannot be used again. Pricing has to be set at a level that will sell the room and you need to be flexible, particularly at the last minute.

Contribution pricing is a term used by financial managers, and the suggestion here is that sometimes a sale will be made where the profit will be minimal. However, the revenue will make a contribution to your fixed costs, which must be paid no matter how much or how little business you have, e.g. rates, insurance, fixed rental charges, etc.

Sometimes, a potential guest will knock at the door and ask the price for a night. When you tell them, they might say that the price is too high. At this point, you should remember the 'fresh cream' concept and perhaps offer a different rate, which might attract them. The counter argument is that it is not fair to the other guests who are paying your full rate. However, consider the contribution to fixed costs and hopefully a bit more. Remember that every time you fly, the chances are that virtually every customer in the aircraft has paid a different rate!

Your unique selling proposition (USP)

Most businesses try to create a unique selling proposition which tells the potential customer something specific about the business that makes it superior to the competition. When creating the USP part of the process it is important to establish what it is the customers want. It may be something as simple as 'peace and tranquillity', or 'pampering', or 'food like granny made', but whatever it is, it has to be possible to produce it time after time for every guest. If you cannot or do not intend to produce food like granny made, then don't use that as a USP, since it will only create dissatisfaction and, probably, complaints.

The likelihood is that the USP will be used in all your advertising since it sets a tone for your establishment and also enables the guests to conjure up in their mind what it is that you offer.

Advertising: What? Where? When? How and How much?

The aim of advertising is to:

◆ create awareness
◆ gain attention
◆ impart information
◆ create interest

- create desire
- solicit action.

Advertising for a small business can be an expensive proposition. However, it may be necessary to carry out some level of advertising. The reasons for advertising are numerous and it is important to be able to direct marketing towards your target market. This means spending the time and gathering the information so that you know this market and if possible, where they are and in addition, what they read. The objectives of marketing are:

- to increase potential customer awareness of what you have to offer

- to improve customer knowledge and perception of your business

- to increase business at a particular time, i.e. off-season promotion

- to introduce potential guests to the opening of the business or perhaps the reopening following refurbishment, or after new owners have taken over

- to publicise a new service the business is offering.

In Chapter 5, in the section relating to the registration card, I mentioned that you can ask the guests when they check in, how they heard of the property. This will give you a very good idea of what advertising works for you. You can also ask when they telephone to enquire about accommodation. It is important that you know this so you can channel your advertising spending in this direction. If you know that it works, use it again and again. It is often said that 'fifty per cent of advertising works but we don't know which fifty per cent'. If you do know which, you must use it.

Other organisations, such as the national or local tourist authorities will spend large amounts of money to advertise the country, or county, or local area, in which you are situated. Since they are spending so much money, it seems logical for your property to jump on this particular bandwagon and take the benefit of the investment in advertising by them. In our case, we have a national tourist board and a local area tourist board. To be a member of one, you must be a member of the other. Both have very well produced listings of properties within different categories. We advertise in both and we have established, from the guest registration forms, that 70 per cent of all our enquiries come from these sources. If the local office calls for a room for the night, they charge us a fee of 10 per cent of the first night's stay. We have, then, narrowed our focus and in effect use a rifle rather than a shotgun approach by getting directly to people who have selected our region by ordering our local tourist authority publications.

You will be inundated with requests to advertise in this or that publication or directory, and we find it impossible to establish which might be better than the other, and so we use none of them. I did, however, allow myself to be talked into advertising in one of our source regions of the UK in a local publication. When I received my copy as agreed, a pictorial description was used which had been cut and pasted from one of our main advertisements. However, nowhere in the advertisement was our location mentioned, so naturally no contacts came from it. In the original, the area heading was at the beginning of the section in which we were advertising in a book-format publication. That resulted in money down the drain, but we learned from it.

The only other advertising we use is one of the automobile organisations and we also advertise in their Bed and Breakfast Guide. This produces a lesser amount of business but we feel it is quite useful to be in this publication. This organisation also has a booking service which produces occasional bookings, although at a rate of eight per cent plus VAT which has to be paid to the booking service.

> **The key then is to establish where your current guests have learned about you, narrow your focus and advertise in these publications. We have found that using a picture in the advertising, while considerably more expensive, is also a very good attraction for our guests.**

In addition, as you listen to your guests talking about their activities of the day and you hear a recurring theme of how wonderful a certain aspect of your local area is, make use of this information. For example, if they tell you the region offers excellent bird watching or wonderful rambling, research the relevant journals purchased by bird watchers and ramblers, and consider advertising in them.

It makes sense to have good relations with your local tourist office and even to become involved through committee membership if you feel you have the time. In doing this, you get to know the individuals involved, and your face and hopefully your property, becomes known to them. In the off-season, you may invite staff from the office to your property for lunch so that they know what they might be selling for you. Travel agents are often invited on familiarisation trips so that they can sell the product. This is the same concept.

Advertising budget

How much you spend on advertising is a similar question to how long is a piece of string. When I was running larger businesses, I had a rule of thumb, which was that all marketing costs should work out at around 8% of revenue. This translates to a small business running below the VAT level (currently £56,000), spending around £4,000 on marketing costs.

The problem with this formula, however, is that at a time when business is poor and sales are on the wane, then less money is available for marketing purposes when the opposite should probably be the case. The need at this time is to stimulate sales through advertising or other marketing tools. This can be nerve racking and you may feel loathe to spend good money when things are going badly, but the injection of funds at this time could reverse the trend.

The best plan, of course, is to set advertising objectives and to then make decisions on a strategy, which shows what steps to take to achieve these objectives. Costing of the strategy can then be carried out and, if necessary, modified to meet the reality of actual finances available. The objectives might state something like 'a 25% increase in guests from the...... region' or 'a 50% increase in shoulder season business for dinner, bed and breakfast specials'. This suggests target marketing at different times, and this is wise since your earlier research told you that a specific target market exists for this, i.e. people from your target region or existing customers who respond to the loyalty concept.

Media

You may choose, as we do, to spend the majority of your budget in conjunction with your national and local tourist authority, but in addition you may wish to consider using the media to assist in your advertising strategy. When you take over a business you will find that media sales 'consultants' cause you to spend quite some time in answering the telephone. They are generally fairly aggressive and you will spend quite some time saying no.

We will look at each part of the media separately:

Television advertising is very expensive, has a high set-up cost and a long lead or preparation time. It is almost certainly out of your league.

Radio advertising, using local radio stations can be much more personal and can reach out to people who might know you, but it is likely to be more expensive if you are trying to generate new customers. The difficult choice is which local radio station, in which region of the country, and in this instance, you may need to use an agency which will research the listening numbers of the local stations in the specific area you decide to target. Using an agency will increase the cost.

Regional press in an area from which you obtain considerable number of your guests may be a possibility and if successive advertising is done, the price may be discounted. The important part of this is selecting the right newspaper. If you are planning to do this for the future, talk to existing guests from this area and ask what paper they read. Get information from the 'horse's mouth'. There are two possibilities in press advertising. You can go for small classified advertisements, which just tickle the memory of the reader, or you can go for display advertising, which buys so many column inches. For the latter, there is the additional cost of artwork, although nowadays this is less complex, since elements of your brochure could be copied.

Static advertising, such as posters or hoardings in places like underground stations, ferries or on buses may be used, again in target regions. This, of course, can be expensive to set up, although long-term rates may not be so expensive. Signs on your own property can also be considered static advertising and this is mentioned briefly later in this chapter.

Direct mail

Earlier I mentioned that we experimented with a loyalty offer sent directly to former guests, offering an off-season special. This is an example of direct, targeted mail.

Direct mail is generally used when you want to:

◆ Remind people who have previously shown interest in your property that you are still there. An example might be to keep a list of people who have requested a brochure but who did not make a reservation. At the start of the next season, send them a direct mail shot to remind them that you exist and what you offer.

◆ Ask an existing customer to recommend someone else for a reward. Perhaps a 10 per cent reduction on their next stay if the introductee makes a booking.

◆ Make special offers to your customer base, such as the loyalty scheme mentioned earlier.

Direct mail usually takes the form of a personal letter that goes straight to a particular person. The letter should get to the point early and should be presented in short, sharp sentences so that the first sight shows that it is not going to be heavy reading. Remember that people nowadays receive so much junk mail that if it resembles this, then it might not even be opened. A hand-addressed envelope might make it look personal enough to be opened rather than binned. The use of a PS maybe to make the 'crunch' point may well be the winning touch, since people often scan down to see who has written the letter and therefore, they see the PS first.

Publicity

There may be occasions when you can make use of an event or situation to achieve free publicity. However, the event or situation has to be newsworthy enough for the editor of the newspaper or magazine to consider it worthy of publication.

The tools used to obtain publicity are press releases, or feature articles, which have been written, by you or by someone for you, about an event or situation. It might be as basic as the information about you taking over the property, or possibly about the changes to the concept that you wish to make following the takeover.

A press release, which you would prepare and send to the newspaper or magazine, should be short and to the point. The aim is to provide information and facts and should not be story-like. You should include your name and address and other contact points such as telephone number and email address. Use pictures if you can, and if you have a logo, use it.

It may be that you devise a competition for people in the East Midlands with prizes of a week for two with dinner, bed and breakfast. Your competition tickles the imagination of the publisher of the local newspaper for that region and he writes a story about it. The story generates interest and, as people take part in the competition, you obtain addresses and eventually, a winner emerges. (Make sure it is above board and independently adjudicated.) You then have the benefit of repeat publicity when the winner is announced. Once you have established a relationship with the newspaper, perhaps you could offer to write a weekly column about food or cookery or some aspect of hotel management. Your name is to the forefront again.

The key to publicity is that unlike advertising, there is no direct cost.

Newsletter

If you have an interest in writing, and have a computer with relevant software, you may decide that sending a low season newsletter is something that will forge a link with previous guests. This will remind them, in a subtle way, that it is time to consider a holiday for next year.

The newsletter could be chatty about the region, but you could also talk about guests who celebrated an anniversary or a birthday or who did something unusual while staying with you. You could also talk about changes that are taking place in the area, including updating of facilities at some of the attractions, new attractions, and generally anything that will create an interest in the region, and also your property. If you have a scanner, you may be able to put in some pictures of guests, of the property, and even yourselves. Remember that we are in the memory business.

Simple is good and cheap!

As we got to know the area, mainly by listening to our guests about where they go during the day, we visited tourist areas, little restaurants and even antique shops. We generally found that the operators were very happy to take some of our brochures, so that in chatting with their customers, they could recommend us if the customers asked about accommodation. This is an inexpensive method of getting to people who are in the area and who know it. This may not convert into bookings until the next year, but it is yet another string to your bow in reaching people who know your region.

The Internet and websites

Later in this chapter I mention that all collateral materials such as brochures, business cards, letterhead and even envelope stickers should have your email address. In addition, any advertising you do, including any with your local tourist authority, should carry your email address.

While the use of email originally seemed to be the domain of the young, we are finding that many of our older guests and potential guests contact us by email, and the number of enquiries by this means is increasing year on year. The good news about this, of course, is that it works out to be considerably cheaper than using paper, envelope and stamps if the deal can be done there and then. At some point you may have to send a brochure, but at least when the deposit comes in, confirmation of its arrival can be made by email. This is something of a saving. We have also noticed that quite a number of our overseas bookings are happy just to contact via email. This is an even bigger saving on the cost of overseas mail.

The other thing that we have is a page with our local tourist association on the area (town) website, and we give the address of this site in our brochure. Potential guests can look at information about the region and then look us up in places to stay. Here we have information and some photographs of our property.

Every week you will have offers by email from people who will set up a website for you, with prices ranging from £50 to £250, with updating charges annually. It is your decision if you want to go this route, but if you do, be sure that the site is well created, so that the search engines pick up your property with ease. If you have some reasonable computer skills and a scanner, you can obtain guidelines for building your own website, and if you have a quiet time during the year this might be a rewarding project for you. Some of the major search engines even give you the opportunity to do this without charge.

Promotions

There are a number of reasons for using promotions. They are:

◆ to encourage people to try your property who have not tried it before
◆ to increase your business at specific times when business needs a stimulus
◆ to take advantage of special holidays or events – Easter, grouse-shooting season, etc.
◆ to increase length of stay
◆ to increase average spend – possibly through a wine sale promotion
◆ to stimulate repeat business from existing guests (loyalty concept).

I mentioned in the section on cash flow, in the business plan, (Chapter 1) that there are essentially two ways to improve cash flow. These are to reduce expenses or to increase sales. A combination of both would work of course. When you are working on your budget and building the sales picture on a week-by-week basis, you have the ideal situation to be able to spot times when special promotions will be of benefit.

I really believe that the sales budgeting process links hand-in-hand with the marketing plan. As you build one, you build the other. For example, you might be calculating anticipated sales for February of next year and it is a depressing picture. This can be seen from a marketing perspective as an opportunity to develop a special event, or a promotion, which will bring guests to you. In the following sections, there are some thoughts that can be developed to increase business. Have you ever been on a Murder Mystery Weekend? What fun to take part in, but also to organise and present!

A formula often considered in the industry is that for every £ spent on a promotion, it should bring in at least £5 to be worthwhile.

I have mentioned a couple of examples of promotions already in this chapter. Our 'loyalty' promotion, which offers existing guests a special dinner, bed and breakfast rate for two or three nights during our early and late season was quite popular. It made us busier at a time when the season had not yet started or was winding to a close. It was also nice to have time to chat with the guests when things were less busy.

In the section on publicity, I mentioned the idea of a competition to generate interest and obtain 'free' advertising in the form of a story. Such a competition might well generate some business and a more detailed concept could be worked out and used. Another promotion might be to send vouchers to existing guests, one of which they can use, but others that they can pass on to friends and relatives. Your profitability drops but your occupancy rises and you have the opportunity to 'capture' some new guests who might well become repeats.

Consider also, during a traditionally quiet period, offering a special interest week, which can be advertised in the relevant special interest magazine or, since the cost of that might be too great for the limited return, offer it to your repeat guests. Wine tasting, arts and crafts, malt whisky tasting, rhododendrons in May are examples. Such an event might incur the cost of a specialist to take charge, but the return at a quiet period might well be worth the effort. It could also be interesting and fun for you!

One promotion I heard of was a B&B which took a basket of muffins to its local tourist office every morning for a month, a basket that had 'Compliments of. . .'. The local staff enjoyed them, as did many of the tourists who were there looking for accommodation.

The B&B had a busy month and more, since the tourist office staff did not forget that particular B&B.

You may have a property which lends itself to business meetings, and the benefit of having coffee breaks, meals and drinks cannot be underestimated when you take on this type of business. Be sure you have the right licence for this.

Alternatively, you might consider executive retreats, where a group of managers from a company takes over the property for a period and you have to look after all their needs during that time, while they are wrestling with some thorny corporate problem.

What about a family or a group of friends or colleagues taking over your guesthouse for a long weekend during the off-season? They can throw away the car keys and you look after them with sumptuous meals and fine wines, and help them to relax and escape the pressures of everyday life.

The three suggestions above probably do not lend themselves to non-exclusive use of the premises. Such activities will probably take up a lot of your time and there is a danger that if you have two guests who are outside the group, they will get less service and will feel uncomfortable to be there. Do not mix groups with individuals.

Finally, one approach to innovative advertising or promotion might be to give a project to business students at your local college to devise a marketing plan for your business. Talk to your local college head and see what interest there might be in such a project. For college students, a 'real life' project would give them an added interest in their studies, and they might well provide you with an excellent platform on which to build your marketing plan. A little bit of recognition and reward to the students might go down quite well too!

Signs

Signs are very important to you if you rely on passing trade for business. Erection of signs will require planning permission and you should apply for this before putting any up. Signs should be big enough to be read from a distance and should not hold too much clutter of information. State basic and important facts. Show any awards or recognition you have so that they can be seen from afar. Consider lighting so they can be seen in the dark and also consider outside lighting for the property so that anyone who is looking for a place to stay has warning to slow down as they approach the property. Such lighting, if well done, can also be a nice feature for guests who are having dinner. Lighting up the garden area is a nice feature.

Communication: letters and brochures

Any communication to potential guests and guests should be done professionally on business letterhead, with matching envelope. The cost will vary depending on how far you want to go in the preparation; however, there is a certain amount of information that should be available on the letterhead.

The letterhead should make it easy for the guest to communicate with you, therefore there are certain key items which should appear on the heading:

◆ your names
◆ the address of the property including the postal code
◆ telephone number
◆ fax number
◆ email address (remember that communication by email works out considerably cheaper for you)
◆ any other item, such as a line drawing of the property.

How far you go with a brochure has to be your decision. However, it should be remembered that potential guests often contact more than one property when they are planning their holiday. Therefore, what you send should stack up as well as, or better than, the others that drop through their letterbox on the same day.

For this reason, my recommendation to you is to have a professionally prepared brochure made up. The input of information can be yours. However, photographs should be professionally prepared. A professional print company should carry out the production of the brochure.

Having said this, there are many computer software programs with which you can produce a less expensive brochure into which you can scan photographs. I have seen some quite good ones, but I feel I can always spot them, and it strikes me that they usually have some elements to them which come over as an amateur production. This will however be a less expensive option.

When preparing a brochure certain items should be included:

◆ Description of the guesthouse/hotel with a positive and warm description, which may be personalised so that the reader feels they know something about you by reading it.

◆ Description of the local area with mention of closeness to town and other major attractions, which may already have attracted the enquiry.

◆ Directions how to get there and, if space permits, a map.

◆ Details of the amenities of the property as well as the rooms and what they have in them. Information such as availability of hair dryers, hospitality tray, telephone, TV, central heating, private car park, etc. Mention all the benefits to the potential guest.

◆ Details the same as on the letterhead, namely your names (your first names will personalise the brochure and make the guest feel at ease), address, telephone number, fax number, email address.

◆ Any awards such as local tourist board stars, Automobile Association ratings, good food organisation commendations.

◆ Meals offered with any details such as 'local produce'.

◆ As many photographs as you can use to give the viewer a real feel for the property and the surrounding area.

◆ Cancellation policy may be included or may be a separate information piece with the tariff

◆ Tariff or rate sheet.

The tariff and the cancellation policy may be separated and produced on a fold-in flier, since these might change during the life of the brochure. Remember that the setting up of the brochure is the main expense, and ordering large quantities can be made at a greatly reduced price.

Business cards

It may seem a bit of an extra expense to have business cards prepared. However, we have found that departing guests often want to take one with them to pass on to friends, colleagues, etc. This is just what you want, since the very act of passing on of the card means that they spend some time talking about you and your business. You cannot buy advertising like that.

The business card can be a fairly simple, inexpensive item or you can go to the extent of having one made with a picture and quite a bit of detail on the back, similar to a mini brochure. This is more expensive, of course, but may well be useful. The minimal information on the business card would be similar to the letterhead, with all the communication information and possibly a line drawing of the property. This is relatively inexpensive to produce and like the brochure, the more you buy the less expensive the unit cost.

If you go the business card route, get plenty and spread them around. They are a useful marketing tool, so make good use of them. Give them to friends and family to carry with them at all times for passing out to potential customers.

Summary

In this chapter, I have suggested to the reader that the key to successful marketing is to identify the customer's needs, wants and expectations, and to develop the product, whatever that may be, to fit these needs, wants and expectations. Having established this and having developed the product, some methods of reaching the potential market segment have been suggested. The budget for advertising should be set and the most useful advertising for your business should be planned within the budgetary guidelines.

The following are the action steps for Chapter 8:

◆ Identify the current customer profile and decide if this is the market you want to serve.

◆ If not, develop the profile of your customer and research their needs, wants and expectations.

◆ Study quality assurance criteria available from your local tourist authority and evaluate your business based on these criteria.

◆ Prepare a strategic plan to better meet these criteria over time.

◆ Identify or create your unique selling proposition.

◆ Evaluate current advertising, set a budget and plan future advertising.

◆ Study the competition with particular attention to pricing and value.

◆ Investigate gaining maximum benefit from the Internet.

◆ Develop collateral materials including brochures, business cards, letterheads, etc.

CHAPTER NINE

Bookkeeping and Financial Aspects

Dealing with your accountant

No matter how much or how little you know about accountancy, it is wise to select and meet with your accountant as early as possible before you start off in the business to be sure that the information you gather is in the most efficient form for you and for him to deal with. Remember, the more work he has to do, the higher the charge is likely to be, so find out what he wants and supply it in good time.

In addition to what he does for you in producing the final accounts, it is wise to have your business accountant deal with your personal tax. In doing this, he will need the big picture of your income from all sources, and also that of your spouse, assuming that you are running the business as a partnership. Remember that an important role for the accountant will be to minimise the tax that you pay, and so it is vital that he has all the necessary information in time to submit the tax returns. Remember also that tax rules are constantly changing and the accountant must stay up to date on all changes, while you might not. Leave it to the professional!

Whatever you do, know the dates for submission of tax returns, and give yourself deadlines well in advance of these, so that all the necessary information is submitted to your accountant on time.

Value Added Tax

Depending on the type of business you have and the level of business you do, you may be below the threshold for payment of VAT. If you are above the level (presently sales of £58,000) then bookkeeping becomes more complex. Good documentation is available free from Customs and Excise. Their website and contact number is listed in the Appendix at the back of the book.

Profit and Loss Account for Westover Guest House

Sales
Minus cost of sales (consumables, i.e. food, liquor, etc.)
Equals gross profit

Minus expenditure
Telephone
Postage and stationery
Advertising
Motor expenses
Subscriptions and memberships
Repairs and maintenance
Cleaning supplies
Accountancy
Rates
Insurance
Heat and light
Wages
Miscellaneous

Financial costs (loan interest)

Depreciation
Plant and machinery
Fixtures and fittings
Motor vehicles

= **Net profit** (before deduction of tax)

Figure 9.1. A typical profit and loss account.

The formula for computing VAT in theory is simple, in that the tax you receive from your customer, known as output tax, is calculated for the period. Next, the tax that you have paid out to suppliers, known as input tax, is calculated. If the output is greater than the input, you pay the difference. If the input is greater than the output, you claim back the difference. For more details and advice, contact your local Customs and Excise Office. A very good manual is available from the VAT office called The VAT Guide. In addition, discuss this with your accountant, who should also be able to advise you.

Profit and loss account

While it seems illogical, it does make sense to start this section with the end product of keeping books, and that is the production of the profit and loss account.

After receiving all the information you have given him, your accountant will produce for you the profit and loss account. This will indicate all the revenue you have taken during the year as well as all expenses. To simplify things, the expenses are deducted from the revenue to show the profit. A typical profit and loss account for a small business will be presented in a similar way to that shown in Figure 9.1.

The profit and loss account can be varied so that it also becomes a more detailed basis for comparison from year to year. For example, you may wish to separate out heat and light income under three separate headings for oil, gas and electricity, so that if you decide to have a purge on energy costs, you will be able to compare how effective you have been, in the next accounting period.

You may also wish to separate out sales and their relative costs, so that gross profits can be calculated for each section of the business. As an example, you may wish to show room sales, food sales, bar sales, and wine sales separately so that you can monitor profitability within each area. This makes your life slightly more complicated but, once the system is set up, it becomes fairly straightforward. If you wish to separate out food from the room sales, then you must set a 'sales figure' for breakfast which is realistic. You may wish to break down a B&B rate per person of £25 into room sales of £21.50 and the food sales for breakfast as £3.50, as discussed in Chapter 6.

In addition, the costs must be separated into food, bar items and wine, in order to calculate the cost percentages accurately. It is common to use percentages since this is a constant, despite fluctuation in sales levels.

> In order to produce the profit and loss account, you need to give the relevant and precise information to your accountant, and for you this becomes virtually a daily task to record the relevant sales and expenses that occur as you run your business.

A note on depreciation. This shows in the profit and loss account as an expense, although in fact it relates to a drop in value of the assets of the business. Since at some time these assets will need to be replaced, it may be prudent to open a depreciation reserve into which you pay the amount shown in the profit and loss account, for the eventual purchase of these assets, e.g. your next car.

The Inland Revenue advises that you set up a system to record all revenue and expenses. This can be a computer software program or an account book or ledger system. They also recommend that you keep all the necessary records and keep them up to date, rather than leaving everything to the end of the year. In addition, be reminded that all records must be kept for at least five years.

Recording revenue

If you decide that you want to use a computer software system, there are many available. In the main, however, they may be somewhat excessive, in that chances are you will not use the full scope of the software. If you are interested, some of the well-known products are Sage, QuickBooks, Dosh, and Clearly Business. Contact details are in the Appendix.

A simple system can look like the one shown in Figure 9.2 below.

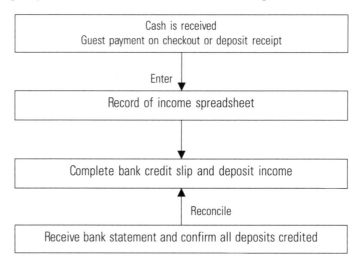

Figure 9.2. A simple system for recording revenue.

My wife and I keep pen and paper records and a simple computer spreadsheet, which are not too extensive, but also give us some statistical information. With each banking, I make an entry on a spreadsheet in the computer, which I call the 'record of income spreadsheet', which has the following headings:

- banking date
- total banked

♦ deposits

♦ accommodation

♦ dinners

♦ bar

♦ telephone calls

♦ cumulative total.

In addition, in order to maintain accurate information on a day-by-day basis, as bank deposits are made, we keep good records on the details of the banking. We do this by using a simple record, which we maintain in a hardback book. This gives us a clear record of who paid what and how, as well as the date it was banked. The detail is as follows:

Guest	Banked	Cheque	Cash	Deposit	Accom.	Dinner	Bar	Phone
Brown	50.00	50.00		50.00				
Smith	170.00		170.00		100.00	64.00	6.00	
May 7	220.00	50.00	170.00	50.00	100.00	64.00	6.00	

The date in the left-hand box of the final line is the date the banking was made, and this will coincide with the deposit as shown in the bank credit slip for the business account.

These, then, are the headings we use and this seems to be acceptable to our accountant. On the profit and loss account for our property, we show total sales and the total costs to calculate gross profit as shown in Figure 9.1. You may wish to separate sales and material costs to show 'departmental' gross profits, as previously discussed.

An example might be as follows:

	Total	Accommodation	Food	Bar items
Sales	45,000	31,000	12,000	2,000
Cost	5,100	0,000	4,000	1,100
Gross profit	39,900	31,000	8,000	900

This separation allows you to make comparisons year on year, and also to calculate food and beverage gross profits separately. Such details enable you to calculate your efficiency year on year. If required, this can be made more accurate by taking monthly stocks of food and beverages. However, this would be a personal decision and not required for final accounts. It would also mean more bookkeeping.

The calculation that involves the use of stocks, also involves careful records and separation of the value of purchases. As an example, the formula for the bar is as follows:

Opening stock (for the period)
Plus purchases (for the same period)
Equals total stock available for sale
Minus closing stock (for the same period)
Equals value of goods sold

Total bar sales
Minus value of goods sold (above calculation)
Equals bar gross profit.

Recording expenses

In order to achieve the above information, accurate records must be maintained regarding all expenditure. As previously mentioned, you can use a computer program for this if you wish. A simple system would look like the one shown in Figure 9.3 below.

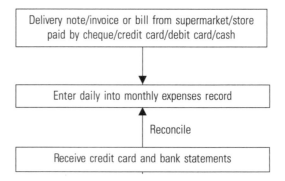

Figure 9.3. A simple system for recording expenses.

The method of recording the expenses is your decision. However, it makes sense to break down the expenses in a similar format to that of the final format of the profit and loss account. Taking into consideration the breakdown of foods, beverages and wine, a record might be kept under the following headings:

◆ telephone
◆ postage and stationery

- advertising
- motor expenses
- subscriptions and memberships
- repairs and maintenance
- cleaning supplies
- accountancy
- rates
- insurance
- heat and light
- wages
- food
- bar items
- wine.

It can be seen that the headings shown here relate to the profit and loss account, although the last three columns give the breakdown for calculating separate gross profits for food, bar items and wine.

For the day-to-day recording of expenses, additional columns would be added, to show date, supplier name and total invoice. However, at the end of the column you might wish to make a note which tells how the invoice was paid, e.g. cheque number, credit card, direct debit or debit card. The column headings might look like this:

Date	Supplier	Invoice total	Telephone	Printing & stat.	Etc....

A further complication might arise when on one invoice or bill you have items, which relate to different headings. This would be dealt with by breaking out the total into the different categories, as shown below:

Date	Supplier	Invoice total	Food	Bar	Wine	Cleaning	Etc....
15.01	Bilko's	£289.41	£107.50	£83.00	£58.91	£40.00	

It is very important that you record sales and expenses on a daily basis.

Using your expenses sheet for the month, when you come back from picking up any supplies or when you write a cheque for a bill, start a new column with the date, the suppliers, separate out the supplies to relevant headings, and complete the entry. It will take a few minutes each day but you will stay up to date. I simply cannot emphasise the importance of this enough. Take care of this aspect of your business for peace of mind.

Clip the invoice or bill to the back of the monthly record and keep every transaction for the current month together. At the end of the month, put all the records and the expense sheet in an envelope and start on the next month. When the bank statement and the credit card bills for that month come in, take an hour or so to check off the entries from the expense sheet and reconcile the statement with the actual expenses incurred. If there are bank debits which do not correspond with the expenses sheet, check it again and if not resolved, query the debit with the bank.

Do not allow this daily routine to falter or you will suddenly be snowed under with a box of bills and invoices, with the further temptation of avoiding dealing with them until the end of the season. The task will then be monumental and you may find errors on the bank statement, which might have become more difficult to investigate.

If you do get behind with this task, be sure to separate the information by month at least so that it is easier to process at a later date.

Petty cash

You may find it useful to pay small bills using cash and to facilitate this, draw an amount, say £100 from the bank, which can be used for such small items. A petty cash record simply shows each transaction, supported by a receipt and an ever-decreasing cash balance. If you take out £10 and have a receipt for £5.75, then put this in the petty cash box with the £4.25 change and record the amount and the supplier from which you made the purchase. You might wish to detail the item. Example:

Petty Cash Analysis for Month of.........			
Date	Supplier	Amount	Balance
1 May 20XX			£100.00
1 May	Bilko's (eggs)	£5.75	£ 94.25

As the initial amount of cash withdrawn is used up, replenish the account by writing a cheque for the amount used and bring the cash available back up to £100. In other words, if you have £3.80 in cash left, write a cheque for £96.20 and take the money from the bank. Enter the £96.20 on the expenses sheet as petty cash. The above sheet with the attached receipts is the justification for this withdrawal.

Balance sheet

A balance sheet shows the financial position of a business at a specific moment in time. It is produced by your accountant at the end of your financial year and in fact relates to the financial position at the date the books were closed. It is conceivable that this could change the following day. The balance sheet is a statement that shows exactly how the business stands, while the profit and loss account shows how it got there. You will be more directly concerned day to day with the data which builds up to the profit and loss account. I note that when I meet with my accountant, our conversations all relate to the profit and loss account and I don't think we have ever discussed the balance sheet.

The accountant will produce the balance sheet and to all intents and purposes, you will not consider this to be a working document as far as day-to-day issues are concerned. The balance sheet shows a balance between the total assets of the business and the total liabilities and net worth.

Two issues arise from the balance sheet, which I feel are relevant to the business. The first is depreciation, which as previously mentioned reduces the value of the fixed assets. The other one, which you will come across when you are buying a business, is goodwill. Goodwill is an intangible asset, which does not appear on the balance sheet, yet is likely to increase the asking price for a property when you are considering buying it. Goodwill has to do with the reputation of the business and possibly its owners.

Budgeting

In the section on the business plan, Chapter 1, I recommended producing a budget for the future to show the lender precisely what you believe the future will hold for your business.

When your business is up and running, the budgetary process should be continued since the budget is a planning and control tool which will help you make decisions for the future. The outline for the budget is the profit and loss account, since the budget relates to sales and expenses.

> **A budget is a plan which estimates how much sales income will be generated, and what expenses will be incurred in order to meet profit requirements.**

Two keys to good budget preparation are firstly, that they should be attainable and secondly, that they do not force standards to drop, e.g. if you cut costs so much that the quality to guests is compromised.

The first part of developing the budget is to calculate sales. This should be built up ideally on a week-to-week basis. You should calculate the likely business you will have daily, how much the guests will spend, and then multiply this up to get weekly, then add together to obtain monthly, and then annual sales estimates.

Let us assume you have six guest rooms, and so for seven days you have 42 possible room sales. If you assume two people in each room, you have 84 bed nights. If your rate for bed and breakfast is £30, then bed and breakfast revenue potential is £2,520.

Now take the first week in March. Look at the number of guests you had last year and ask yourself if for any reason you expect more. Make a conservative decision at this stage and calculate the bed and breakfast sales for the week. Let's assume you expect to use two rooms at double occupancy for six nights. This calculates out to be 24 bed nights at £30, which brings in £720.

Now you need to add in the anticipated sales of dinners, and drinks consumed with dinners. Hopefully you have kept some statistics, which give you a 'capture' rate for dinners. This means the number of guests who are in-house that have dinner. We find out that the 'capture' rate is different for different months, so be sure to keep percentages for each month. If the percentage of guests that have dinners in March is 60 per cent, then you can put in a rate of 24 (guests) times 60 per cent, which suggests that 14.4 people will have dinner. Take the round 14 and multiply this by the price of your dinner, let's say £16. You can then calculate the dinner sales for that week. This totals £224 for dinners.

Next you have to calculate how much you will take in the bar and wine sales. Again have statistics that will help you. Have a statistic of beverage sales as a percentage of food sales, and then multiply this out. We find that for every £100 of food that we sell, we sell about £20 of wine or drinks. This then will translate in the calculation to be 20 per cent of £224, which means beverage sales of £45.

So now we have the following sales figure for the first week of March:

	£
Accommodation sales	720
Dinner sales	224
Beverage sales	45
Total sales for week 10 of year 20XX	989

While this seems like a lengthy process, it has the added advantage of you becoming very familiar with the plan for your business. As mentioned in Chapter 1, the calculation of the original budget plan for presentation to the lender creates invaluable information to enable you to present a business plan confidently.

If your business is seasonal then clearly, the seasonal aspects of the business should be taken into consideration, but perhaps you see the advantage of extending your season. From a marketing standpoint, as you identify periods of low business in the budget, you would want to develop promotions for this period in order to improve the sales as explained in Chapter 8.

The next part is to estimate expenses. As you gain more knowledge of your business, you will identify areas where you want to make improvements, and develop a strategy which will assist with this. Energy management might be just such an area. Certain costs are fixed costs, which cannot be changed, while other costs vary according to volume of business. Control of variable costs is vital to protect your profit margin.

It is simple to calculate all expenses for the previous period as a percentage of sales, and many businesses simply calculate the expense as a percentage of the new sales figure. A more efficient way is for you to work out each expense in terms of money to be spent, and create the actual cost figure. In this way, you are setting yourself a cost target and you are more likely to work towards achieving this cost. As you develop the expenses part of the budget, keep asking yourself how you can reduce costs without reducing standards and value for your guests.

If you find you have been ultra conservative or optimistic with your budget, make a quarterly revision. Most companies do this and it makes good sense to work to accurate predictions.

- Appoint an accountant, ideally with small hotel accounts experience.

- Before opening a bank account, ask questions relating to bank charges and compare different bank charges.

- Establish with your accountant whether or not VAT registration is necessary.

- Devise a system to record revenue.

- Devise a system to record expenses.

- Set up a petty cash system.

- Make a decision regarding the acceptance of credit cards.

- Promise yourself to keep up to date with your bookkeeping records by spending a few minutes each day on this task.

CHAPTER TEN

Ancillary Departments

Many people going into a small business do not give any thought to the technical and mechanical aspect of running the business. It can come as a bit of a shock when things begin to go wrong or problems arise which they are unable to solve easily. In Chapter 2, I made mention of the benefits of taking over a property which is in pristine condition. However, that is not to say that things can't go wrong the very next day.

To some extent your background experience, or at least your interest in technical things, will be a significant factor in staying on top of this important aspect of running your small hotel or guesthouse.

I have a friend who owns a guesthouse nearby who previously was an engineer, and there are so many times that I envy his expertise and ability. When faced with a technical problem in his property, he is able to analyse the problem, and then he is personally able to implement the solution. The other aspect also is the joy of not having to deal with tradesmen who, in my experience, promise the world and often, deliver very little. I apologise here and now if I offend the good tradesmen out there, but I have to say some recent experiences with them have caused me great frustration in running my small property.

As you have no doubt gathered, I have no experience or ability in technical areas. My wife is much more competent than I am but, more importantly, she is so much more patient in taking the time to try to work out the problem. This I feel is a key to getting things done, thereby saving time, frustration and money. Quick decisions are sometimes regretted, so it is useful to apply a process when things go wrong.

The problem-solving process

This is a process, which can be used for problem solving when something goes wrong, or when you feel that change is necessary. By applying this process, you may find that there is a relatively simple solution which you have the ability to implement.

Step One: Identify the problem. Ask yourself 'What do we want to change?' Know in your mind what will be happening when the problem is solved.

Step Two: Ask 'What is stopping us from getting it the way we want it to be?' List the main causes, with the most important at the top and then in descending order of importance.

Step Three: Generate potential solutions and list the solutions.

Step Four: Select the best solution(s). Ask yourself 'What is the best way to achieve the result we are looking for?'

Step Five: Implement the solution.

Step Six: Evaluate the effects of the solution. Ask 'Is this how we wanted it to be?'

This process can be used for any problems which exist in your property, including staff problems. It achieves quality results and is best used as a brainstorming approach with as many people as possible getting involved. It will help you make decisions in many situations by going through a systematic process. If the problem is a technical one where you do not have a great deal of expertise, you can go as far as you can before calling a tradesperson and then together, you can follow the process to reach the ideal solution.

Public utilities, energy and other systems

Most small property operators are not aware that there are so many different systems within the property that need to be cared for and nurtured to ensure they operate on a 24 hours a day, seven days a week basis. These may include:

◆ heating, ventilation and perhaps, air conditioning
◆ lighting systems
◆ fire protection systems
◆ hot and cold water systems
◆ refrigeration and freezers
◆ telephone systems
◆ television, cable satellite systems
◆ sewage system – perhaps septic tank.

Fire protection systems

Fire safety is a major concern for all operators in the hospitality industry and to take the line of least resistance is certainly not the sensible way to go. Your local fire safety officer will inspect your property and will advise you on what steps must be taken to ensure that it meets the requirements of the necessary legislation. The relevant act is the Fire Precautions Act, 1971.

I have already suggested that prior to purchase, you and your lawyer should have sight of the fire certificate that has been issued for the property. It might even make sense to visit the fire chief in order to establish whether any changes might be required with the change of ownership. At this time also, you will be able to establish if the legislation is likely to change in a way which might require major alterations after you take over. If this is the case, it might be possible to have the cost estimated and to use this when negotiating a price for the property. This has the effect of sharing the cost between the old and the new owner.

If your property permits smoking, it is even more important to be vigilant and to install smoke and heat detectors, which may be in addition to the fire alarm system already installed. Consult your local fire brigade for their professional advice.

Your local fire safety officer will contact you with general advice and will require you to test equipment on a weekly basis, as well as carrying out fire drills with staff and possibly guests. Be aware that if you are negligent in making checks, you have effectively broken the law and, if a tragedy occurs, you are likely to be deemed to be liable. Advice generally will relate to:

◆ Keeping fire doors shut when not in use to prevent the spread of heat and smoke.

◆ Ensuring that final exit doors can be readily opened from the inside without the use of a key and keeping the outside area clear for evacuation.

◆ Keeping corridors and stairways clear.

◆ Ensuring exits are clearly marked and visible.

◆ Ensuring the fire alarm is in working order (check weekly). Train staff to recognise the alarm and know what to do in case of an alarm.

◆ Being sure that staff know where fire extinguishers are and how to use them.

♦ Having emergency lighting checked and maintained regularly and immediately replacing spent bulbs.

♦ Being sure that staff are aware of their responsibilities in the case of fire. They should know how to raise the alarm; how to call the fire brigade; when not to tackle a fire; how to use the right fire extinguisher correctly and the correct evacuation procedures for the property.

♦ Making guests aware when they arrive of the action to take in the case of fire. This should be described on back of bedroom door.

♦ Checking electrical wiring regularly. (Preventive maintenance.)

♦ Keeping portable heating devices away from furniture and combustible materials.

♦ Keeping open fires guarded and having chimneys swept regularly. (Preventive maintenance.)

♦ Checking smoking areas regularly and providing adequate ashtrays. Checking for lighted cigarette ends last things at night.

♦ Not allowing a build-up of rubbish, which tends to be highly flammable.

♦ Keeping aerosols away from direct heat. Do not store in the kitchen.

While the above list is not exhaustive, it gives general guidelines. However, check for the advice from your local fireofficer, and comply with the advice given by your local brigade. It is vital never to shortcut any requirement for fire safety for your guests, your staff, your property and yourself.

Professionals should carry out preventive maintenance of all fire safety equipment and a record should be maintained of all work carried out in your equipment log. The national companies tend to operate in all areas. However, you may prefer to seek out the locally based fire engineering company to ensure a quick response when problems occur.

Another requirement by your local fire brigade will be to carry out a fire risk assessment. Essentially, this will require you to:

♦ identify fire safety hazards

♦ decide who might be harmed and how

♦ evaluate the risks arising from the hazards and decide whether existing precautions are adequate and appropriate

♦ record the findings of the assessment and action taken

♦ review the assessment from time to time and revise if necessary.

Finally, in considering aspects of fire precautions, it is vital to point out that close cooperation with the local fire brigade can help you, and save you time and money in making your property safe. Consider them as the experts and get it right.

Energy management

There are numerous ways in which energy costs can be measured. Large hotel corporations will measure energy costs as a cost per occupied room and will use this as a comparative base. Others will use cost per square foot/yard/metre. Many companies simply calculate the energy cost as a percentage of sales.

Whatever method you employ, it should be used as a comparative base from year to year and as a target or challenge to improve in the future. Having said that of course, there is a danger that in trying to reduce this cost, the service to the guest may be compromised. Perhaps the heat is not adequate or the light bulbs at the bedsides are so dim that it is impossible to read.

It is clear that there are benefits to effective energy management. Reduced usage of electricity, gas and oil means reduced bills for these utilities. Monitoring and comparing these costs year on year, based on the comparable periods will help you target the problems and reduce the costs.

> The public at large is becoming more aware of green and environmental issues and they are your customers. They may well be more interested in staying at a property, which conforms to their ideals in terms of energy management and green issues.

VisitScotland has a Green Tourism Business Scheme devised to help businesses working in the hospitality sector to gain benefits by managing their environmental responsibilities and there are likely to be similar initiatives in other regions throughout the country.

At a cost, it is possible to bring in an energy consultant who will survey your property and will make recommendation for savings. If this is an independent, there will be a cost for the consultation. If they are a supplier, they will be trying to make a sale. You must decide which way you want to go. It may be that you will be happy to research the topic and make the necessary changes yourself.

Certainly consider having an expert look at the insulation of your property to see if there is an expensive loss of heat. This can be one of the big loss areas, as can be single plate glass in windows. While the cost of installation of double or triple glazing can be expensive, the running cost of energy and the added value to the property might well make it worthwhile.

In order to reduce energy costs, the concept of energy management should be applied and strategies introduced to make the changes. As previously mentioned, knowing what the costs are period by period, is important. Knowing the actual basis for the costs also becomes important. What is the cost per unit? What is the contract cost? We find that we are inundated with calls from companies which want to take over our electricity charging and who offer all sorts of special and 'competitive' rates. Perhaps they are and perhaps not. It is important to ask all the right questions, including what is the cost per unit, the added contract cost per period and, indeed, whether there are any additional costs. Finally, find out how easy it is to get out of the contract in case you find it is not improving your energy cost.

If you have staff, training is important so that the staff also implement the savings you devise for your property. Communicate what you are aiming to achieve in terms of energy cost and make them part of the challenge.

Inefficient equipment uses more energy and so the application of a preventive maintenance programme will help reduce energy costs. More information regarding a preventive maintenance programme will appear later in this chapter. Investment in low energy light bulbs will also reduce running costs and replacement costs, although the initial investment will be quite high.

In addition to the above, there are a number of simple, small things, which can be done, and the many small savings might well make a considerable overall saving when aggregated. Some simple and seemingly obvious suggestions are:

◆ Turn off equipment such as coffee machines and coffee machine hot plates when not in use.

◆ Use cold water instead of hot when cold will do the job, e.g. washing machines when laundering lightly soiled items.

◆ If cooking with electricity, make sure the pans have a flat bottom for maximum contact.

◆ Use pot lids to increase the heat and when boiling, lower the temperature.

◆ Use thermostats accurately to obtain optimum temperature rather than excess.

◆ Fit accurate thermostats with gauges to radiators.

◆ Thaw frozen foods in the refrigerator. This is good hygienic practice but also the cold of the freezer item causes the temperature to drop and the refrigerator to switch off.

◆ Do not put hot items in the refrigerator.

◆ Ensure that the seal doors on refrigerators and freezers are good.

◆ Do not clean or peel vegetables under running water.

◆ Towards the end of season, when possible, clear and switch off unnecessary freezers.

◆ When using a dishwasher, only wash with a full load.

Maintenance

The aim of maintenance is to keep an item of equipment in its original state and to stop it depreciating or failing. Clearly, certain pieces of equipment have heavy usage and decline is to some extent inevitable. To take the analogy of a car however, it can be seen that a car which is not cared for will deteriorate faster than one which is cared for and regularly serviced. Herein lies the basis for an effective system of preventive maintenance.

Before discussing this in more detail, it should be pointed out that it is sometimes possible to have maintenance contracts on certain items of equipment. Generally, the terms of such contracts are that there are a predetermined number of service calls, sometimes with a special rate for labour, but with charges for parts. Such a contract might mean priority call-outs in case of emergency and a reduced labour charge for such events. Such a contract may be worth considering if the life of the item of equipment is prolonged. We have a service contract for our heating boiler as it is an essential piece of equipment with which we do not want to have problems.

Tools, equipment and supplies

No matter how non-technical you might be, it is wise to have a selection of tools, which will help to make the job easier. Remember that some tasks which you can carry out, may take you much longer than an expert, but you must consider the cost you save by doing it yourself. If the equipment you have is user friendly, and uses power to save muscles, then learn how to operate it correctly. A local college might well offer DIY courses which will help you gain technical ability and, most importantly, confidence to tackle more jobs around the guesthouse/hotel.

> Have a place set aside for your tools and equipment, and have the storage areas marked so that when anything is used it is replaced in the right section. Remember that at some point you may have a panic situation, or limited time, and you do not want to be getting frustrated searching for the correct tools for the job.

Keep a stock of supplies you are likely to need, such as rawlplugs, screws, nails, wire, string, and so on. Consider also electrical supplies such as plug fuses, batteries, and electrical fuses if your property uses them, and a selection of light bulbs to fit all your needs. Consider over time switching to energy-efficient light bulbs which, although expensive initially, pay off handsomely in terms of operating and replacement cost.

Keep a record of where you buy each of these items, and also the price paid, so that you get a feel for the inflationary aspect of the items, which have no direct revenue return. These are the costs which will eat into your profit if you do not take steps from time to time to adjust the sales price to account for increases. Listing the name of the supplier is useful for items you do not purchase often. It saves time and confusion to be able to look up where to buy the supplies that you need only occasionally, when you cannot remember where you bought them.

Preventive maintenance

Preventive maintenance is a process you go through in order to prolong the life of a piece of equipment, to keep it at its optimum efficiency and to eliminate, as far as possible, the chance of the equipment breaking down.

Again, the best analogy is what we tend to do with our car in that we make sure it is well serviced, according to the manufacturer's instructions at the prescribed times. In addition, when setting out on a long journey, we go through a number of checks in the hope of limiting the possibility of any kind of breakdown problem. Similarly, at the start of our busy season, we go through a process of checks to make sure that we minimise the possibility of breakdowns in our property during the busy period.

Key to good preventive maintenance is that when a piece of equipment is purchased or a new boiler or heating system is installed, all the instructions and manuals are not only kept, but are read and used. When reading the manual, it may be possible to create from it a checklist of times when certain steps should be taken to maintain the piece of equipment. With complex equipment, it will require technical people to carry out this maintenance. However, your responsibility is to call them in at the relevant time for the work to be done. Not too soon, as this is causes extra expense, but not too late so that there is a possibility of a breakdown. This suggests a simple record of all the equipment with perhaps a page in a file for each one with something like the following information:

Preventive Maintenance Record		
Equipment: Mower	Purchase date: 07.99	Maker: XYZ
Task:	Date for work:	Date of work:
Service	Every mid-May	
Check plug	Every 3 months	

Simpler pieces of equipment can be dealt with in-house by you, or by a handyman who comes in from time to time, at your request, to carry out simple preventive maintenance tasks. An example of this would be with a vacuum cleaner, which has to have the dirt bag or the drum emptied when full, but which will also need belts to be changed after a period of time before they break down due to constant use, thereby causing a panic situation at that time. Six-monthly cleaning of the drum, according to manufacturers' instructions, is another example.

This process can be simplified by you, by not only preparing a schedule of preventive maintenance, complete with dates for the year, but also step-by-step instructions on what must be carried out. This is worth the effort if you prolong the life of the item and also, if it eliminates a panic situation if the breakdown occurs. Remember Murphy's Law, which says, 'If things can go wrong, they will go wrong and at the worst possible time!'

Handyman duties

It is possible that you may be lucky enough to obtain the services of a handyman who is likely to be self-employed. What you obtain from this person should complement your skills and weaknesses. In other words, if you are competent in the area of gardening, then this need not be one of their skills. If you are weak in terms of fixing things and plumbing, then these should be their strong areas. Such a person would be on-call both for emergencies, and for planned work which you discuss and plan with them to suit their and your timetable.

Remember that in securing the services of such a person you should look at their abilities within the range of skills that may be needed. Bear in mind repairing light equipment, electrical tasks, joinery tasks, plumbing tasks, tiling and roofing tasks, and possibly general gardening or garden repair tasks.

Such a person is a gem and if you can find one, you will be lucky. Failing that, you need the services of tradesmen within the various disciplines as outlined above.

Dealing with tradesmen

The alternative to the handyman is using local tradesmen, and herein lies a major problem from what I see and hear. My experience is that most tradesmen are busy, but they do not want to turn down business, so they will say that they will do the job, but then do not show up when they said they would. Alternatively, they will start the job and then not follow through, so the job remains half finished. There seems to be a tendency to start many jobs and just keep the plates spinning, causing headaches for all the clients.

The problems you will face relate not only to dealing with emergencies but also to getting planned work carried out.

To find local tradesmen, contact the local Chamber of Commerce who will be able to give you the address of members within the section, and this is a start in finding the help you might need.

It is important to find out who the best tradesmen are and try to meet with them even at a time when no work needs to be done. You are trying to build a relationship, which you hope will help build loyalty from the person. Initially talk to local people, and also obtain information from the person from whom you bought the property . They are likely to tell you who to use and who not to touch, from their own experience. Remember that such a reference means that these are people who know your property and this might be very useful, saving you time and expense.

Ask questions in the local hardware store and building supplies depot since they deal with the tradesmen on a daily basis and they also know who has the most business, which is a good indicator of ability and reliability, as well as possible price.

If possible ask the tradesman for reference, i.e. names and addresses of people they have done work for, and call them. They are more likely to be honest during a telephone call. If your project is a big and costly one, ask if you can see the job that was done and try to establish if it was indeed done well.

Whatever you do, do not pay cash up front. If a builder needs cash up front to buy materials, it must make you wonder what kind of state the business is in.

Major projects

In the case of any major projects being undertaken, for example re-roofing or building en-suites, it makes good sense to contact three possible contractors and ask for a quotation. When you do this, be sure that the work they bid for in their quotation is the same for all three contractors. This means that you should prepare a detailed description of what needs to be done and on which you are expecting the contractors to quote. If technical information needs to be given, ask an expert to help you with the technical jargon and description.

Remember that sometimes the lowest quotation does not offer the best result, and again, you should ask someone who may be more technical than you are to help you analyse the quote.

I have recently been gathering quotes for the facia and downpipes for our property. I have had three quotes and all seem outrageous. However, one of them was even offering to replace the existing facia in what transpires to be an illegal way, without the necessary ventilation. I know this because I asked an expert. If I had gone ahead, future buyers might find this out through the survey and might well try to force down my selling price. Consult experts where high-cost work has to be carried out.

Beware of high-level spending which will only put limited value on your property. An example of this might be the building of a rather expensive conservatory for use as a lounge. This could mean that the spending might not be recouped on sale of the property. If the conservatory costs you £45,000 the question is whether the selling price of your property has risen by £45,000 after it has been built. On the other hand, it might mean that you are able to increase room rates, thereby gaining benefits in the operation, which will show up on the profit and loss account. It is necessary to balance one with the other over a period of time.

Gardening

The garden of your property can be a source of pride and perhaps accomplishment for you, a pleasure to your guests and perhaps even a way of reducing costs for the business. From simple but attractive window boxes, which give a cared-for look, to cobbled courtyards with hanging gardens and a blaze of colour, you can make your garden a major feature.

From the gardening point of view, the appeal of the property we eventually purchased was that it was attractive, varied, well shaped, colourful and had good ground cover requiring not too much attention. We saw it at slightly different times of the year and felt that from a guest point of view it had an appeal and lots of variety of colours. In the fullness of time, we have found that it is a relatively easy garden to maintain even during the busiest months with only an hour to spare here and there, and in fact, this is what we had hoped would be the case.

The question of the size of the garden and the need for attention is a crucial one. In Chapter 2, I gave some information about a friend who spends a considerable amount of time in his garden, but does not serve dinners. This is an option. However, it is one which perhaps limits revenue opportunities. The alternative may be to find a simple garden, but this may reduce the ambiance for the guests. To some extent it depends on the activities of the guests and whether they are likely to take advantage of your garden by sitting there or taking a walk.

One option might be to have a large garden, which needs a lot of attention, for which you hire the services of a part-time gardener or of a contractor who will be contracted to carry out certain aspects of the garden work throughout the seasons.

The only major work that we have had done by a contractor was the cutting of a rather high hedge which comprised many different bushes and trees, including some rather established, fast-growing trees. This required equipment and know-how, so we elected to pay for that service rather than hire or purchase the equipment.

It may also be possible to find a retired neighbour who likes gardening and who would be happy to potter and keep your garden tidy for a small consideration.

Preparing hanging baskets is time consuming, but this work is generally carried out before the season becomes very busy. Our local garden centre offers a service of taking barrels and containers in the spring and filling them and basically setting up the colour scheme in the pots for the season. This is a useful service if gardening is not your 'thing'. Consider having a discussion with your local garden centre people to see what services they offer that might release your time for other things. It is of course an additional expense.

You may feel that a vegetable garden is important, and even a greenhouse in which you can produce herbs, fruits and vegetables for use in the kitchen. This certainly would have an appeal for the guests and might well be used as a USP in advertising and the brochure. This is a considerable issue for many guests, as we know from the on-going move towards organic and 'home grown' foods. Here again, the possibility of a reduction in costs of food due to using 'home' produce might apply. Given the low cost of many imported products in supermarkets nowadays, this might be debatable. Freezing enables a glut of a certain vegetable to be preserved for use in soups, pâtés and purées in the future. A fruit and vegetable garden, however, can be time consuming to look after.

> One area where costs can be reduced, however, is likely to be in the availability of flowers from the garden for the dining room, the bedrooms, bathrooms and the public area. If purchased from a florist or even the supermarket, this may be quite an expense. However, if you plan for a good supply of colour to be available throughout the year, savings can be considerable.

Whatever the case with gardens, the trap you should not fall into is saying that you feel you will cope, and then find that in high season, you are just keeping your head above water in the house, while the grass is growing, flowers need dead heading and the garden is just beginning to look a bit unkempt. While you might turn the other way and hope it is not really happening, the guests will certainly see it.

Painting and decorating

Earlier I mentioned that maintenance is to do with keeping an item in its original state and preventing it from deteriorating. Painting and touching up on an ongoing basis, keeps the property looking in pristine condition. Be sure to look at your property from the eyes of the guests and see the start of deterioration. Fix it as soon as possible on a temporary basis and, at the first opportunity, complete the job more permanently.

There are two areas of need within the painting and decorating area, namely inside and outside the building. Planning is the key for the inside, and if you have six rooms, a good rotation for decorating might be to work on one room a year and do what you feel is necessary for the décor. At the end of our first year, we spent about £1,000 redecorating and buying new furniture and bed linens for one of our twin rooms. We did the painting ourselves and saved some cost because of that. Our repeat guests were thrilled with the changes and so that is our plan, to work on a room every year.

In addition, however, it is wise to keep some of the paint you have used in order to be able to touch up scrapes and scratches from cases and occasional moving of furniture for deep cleaning.

The same applies to public areas, which get lots of wear and tear. Stay vigilant and look around through other people's eyes in order to see things which are getting shabby and in need of a touch-up. Touch up at the first available opportunity, even if it means after the guests have left the lounge at 11.00p.m. in order to avoid guests touching wet paint.

In Chapter 4, we looked at the methods used by quality advisors and one of the areas they are concerned with is the exterior of the building. This needs care and attention for an overall good impression.

If the property has a rendered covering which has been painted, then this is likely to need freshening after the winter period when there is likely to be a mossy covering. A good power hose is usually enough to solve this problem. However, a plan to repaint should be made and budgeted for as this can be a fairly extensive project. As mentioned earlier in this chapter, this would be a case for obtaining alternative bids from different contractors.

It is important to keep outdoor signs fresh and clean: it is possible that these should be washed or even touched up on an annual basis. Remember that signs may be the first impression as people drive along. If they indicate a cared-for look, they might drive in and not by.

Summary

While this area of operation seems remote from the real business of running a small hotel or guesthouse, if not set up properly, it can become a problem area and a considerable cost. This chapter has aimed to help remove the irritation of unexpected and time-consuming problems cropping up at awkward times. It has highlighted some aspects of energy management which little by little can reduce your utility bills.

The following are the action steps for Chapter 10:

- Before the vendor leaves, have a conversation with them about the local tradesmen and their strengths and weaknesses.

- Before the vendor leaves ask for all manuals and instruction books for equipment.

- Set up a preventive maintenance schedule.

- Create an emergency list of plumber, electrician, etc.

- In first three months, make decisions regarding use of handyman, gardener, etc.

- Set up workshop/tool/equipment/replacements (e.g. light bulbs) storage area.

- Carry out fire risk analysis.

- Have all fire prevention equipment checked and serviced if necessary.

- Carry out an energy usage survey and set up an energy policy.

CHAPTER ELEVEN

Staffing

As previously mentioned in this book, an important decision you will have to make is whether or not you will have any staff to help you to run your business. This is important since, from one point of view, you will increase your costs and possibly create a distance between yourself and your guests, but on the other hand, you will give yourselves more time to enjoy a life outside the business. The decision is yours.

Generally speaking, I would say that a business greater than six letting rooms is likely to need some additional staff in order to maintain a standard that will be acceptable to your guests. A property smaller than six letting rooms might well need to have some additional help. This will depend on the amount of time taken for tasks like gardening, and even travelling time for the purchase of foodstuffs etc.

There is another possibility, which is that if the food side of the business is a big factor and if you feel you do not have the culinary skills to make it work, you may feel you have to hire a professional. Depending on the size of your business, this might be too expensive but, certainly, it may be something that has to be considered.

If you have 'taken over' staff from the previous owners, then you have a legal commitment to them. There is a regulation which covers this called the Transfer of Undertakings (Protection of Employment) Regulations 1981, and further details of your responsibilities and the rights of the employees, can be obtained from the Department of Trade and Industry in their booklet PL699 which can be obtained from JobCentres. Clearly, if you are taking over staff, it is wise to discuss with the vendor what their strengths and weaknesses are, and possibly to meet and 'interview' them prior to the takeover. This is not really an interview situation since they have continuity of employment, but it is helpful to get things off on the right foot. There is a possibility that an employee may not wish to continue under the new circumstance, and if this is the case, you should obtain a resignation in writing from them.

Recruitment

The conventional methods of recruitment might not necessarily be relevant to your situation. The cost of advertising may well be prohibitive and the use of an agency is also a costly alternative. Since you are likely to want someone who can be 'on call' on occasions, it is wise to try to find staff who live near to your business. The logical way of making contact with them in this case is through a local institution such as the local JobCentre, placing a card in the local store or supermarket, or simply by using word of mouth, and letting neighbours and local shopkeepers know that you are looking for someone.

Defining the job

It is important before you start the recruitment process that you become clear in your mind what you will want the employee to do for you. Not only what, but when and at what level of business. In order to decide this, you and your partner need to sit down and brainstorm the tasks that need to be carried out. Decide what you feel you must do and then begin to allocate the tasks which can be carried out by an employee. When you have a list of tasks, then you have a basis for a job description. The job description will be simplified by linking together related tasks to form duties and the core element of the job description will be a list of duties. In addition, a job description will have a job title; a section for the 'scope and general purpose' of the job, and possibly the hours of work, if this can be defined well enough. The job description then is likely to look something like the one shown in Figure 11.1.

A job description should not go into too much detail, but should be sufficiently detailed that the employee knows what they have to do. The exercise you go through to produce it helps identify your role and the employee's role.

You may wish to also produce a job specification, which describes what you are looking for in the employee who will take the position. In this, you can describe the qualification required to be able to do the job. You may, for example, specify that some heavy lifting is necessary, bending and kneeling, as well as describing the previous job experience that the employee should have. You might also want to describe the personality type ideally suited for guest contact. However one must be careful not to use this to discriminate.

Job Description

Job Title: Guesthouse Housekeeping Assistant

Hours of Work: 10.00a.m. to 2.30p.m., 6 days per week.

Scope and General Purpose: To assist the owners with housekeeping duties after guests leave, and prepare bedrooms and public areas for new arrivals and returning guests.

Duties:

Routine: **Occasional**:
Stripping beds   Shampooing carpets
Remaking beds   Touching up paint in rooms
Cleaning shower
Cleaning toilet
Dusting room
Polishing mirrors and glass in bedrooms and public areas
Vacuuming bedrooms, hallways and public rooms
Replacing used room amenities
Dusting lounge and dining room
Ironing sheets and pillowcases

Figure 11.1 A typical employee job description.

The use of the two documents can be seen if you consider someone sitting in front of you who is applying for the job. Now you can see that the job specification tells you the physical requirements of the job as well as the experience you are looking for, while the job description enables you to ask questions to ascertain the ability of the applicant to carry out the job, and possibly also whether the job is truly what the applicant is looking for. These two documents clarify the search for the ideal applicant.

The advertisement

When preparing an advertisement for use perhaps in the local store, or supermarket, or even in preparing the information you give to the JobCentre, be sure it is complete. The details should include:

◆ the job; the scope and general purpose from the job description will help here

◆ the hours of work and days per week

◆ the location

◆ any benefits such as meal, uniform, etc

◆ the rate of pay

◆ the person to contact and the full address and telephone number.

If you are competing with others, try to make your advertisement look distinctive and attractive so that immediately, the applicant gets a favourable impression of your property. Use your logo if you have one.

It may be useful to have a simple one-page application form which you can ask the applicant to fill in, either by sending it to them, or by having them fill it in before the interview. This is a useful document to start the employee record if indeed the person is hired. Information likely to be useful is as follows:

◆ name

◆ address

◆ telephone number for contact

◆ previous similar experience and where

◆ relevant qualifications if any

◆ name and telephone number of work-related reference

◆ how soon the person can start work.

While this information is not too in-depth, it will give you an idea about whether you are looking at a short or longer training situation.

The interview

When a potential applicant has made contact, arrange to meet at a time which is convenient to you, particularly when the pressure is off, and when you have enough time to do justice to the interview process. In our industry, potential employees are frequently put off from the start when the interviewer is not available, and not prepared due to pressure of business. The same applies for employees as for guests, in that 'you only get once chance to make a good first impression'. For employees, it often starts badly and goes downhill from there onwards. Do not let this happen.

Have a quiet area set aside for the interview. Have the job description and the job specification available for your use, and have a copy of the job description available to give to the applicant. Before the interview, jot down a few pertinent questions that you need to ask about the core aspects of the job and about previous experience.

When the applicant arrives, welcome them warmly and make them comfortable by chatting. This can perhaps be done as you walk them round the property, effectively introducing them to your standard of operation.

Following the walkabout, sit down in the prearranged area and begin the interview. Remember that an interview is a two-way street and you should give the applicant the opportunity to ask you questions. Remember also that you gain information from listening to the applicant so let them talk. A good ratio is that you talk 20 per cent of the time and the applicant talks 80 per cent of the time. The way to get the applicant to talk is by asking open-ended questions rather than questions that have a yes/no answer. For example 'Did you enjoy your last job?' is a yes/no question. A better approach would be 'What did you like most and least about your last job?' This will encourage the candidate to talk and you learn something about them.

In this process, you are hoping to learn if they are capable, flexible and prepared to do the job as you described it, and most importantly, you want to find if they are compatible with your team. You want good rapport and a good relationship within your small team. Be looking for hints that will tell you the best applicant from this standpoint. If there is an applicant with limited experience but who will fit in with your team, then remember that you can train to your standard, and this might be the best option for harmony in your workplace.

The last part of any interview is to give the applicant a chance to ask you any questions and to answer them. Then explain the next step. If you have others to interview, explain that you will call by tomorrow afternoon, or whatever, and do it. Make your decision. Contact all applicants. Thank all for attending and ask the unsuccessful candidates if you can keep details on file in case something crops up at a later date. Maintain good relations with all since who knows when you might wish to talk to them again.

One final thought regarding employment, and this has to do with the qualifications and skills an applicant presents to you. It may well be that you identify excellent skills presented to you by the applicant, so you might feel that it is possible to adjust your role, and that of your spouse/partner, to accommodate the skills presented by this particular potential employee.

Following the interview, it is wise to take references from previous employers, and my experience is that a telephone call is the most effective way to do it. Ideally speak to the direct supervisor of the employee and ask questions to establish how similar that job was to the one you have available and how effectively the person coped with the work. It is wise to establish what kind of team player the employee was, as well as their attitude to guests. You may want to ask if they would rehire this employee, as this can give a real insight into the work and attitude of the employee.

Arrange to meet again briefly with the successful applicant to finalise details and to arrange a starting date and time. At this time, you may wish to give the employee a contract of employment. This is a required legal document, which outlines certain necessary information for the employee. The aforementioned job description is a part of the document and other required sections are as follows:

- the employer's name and address
- the name of the employee
- the job title and job description
- the starting date
- the rate of pay and when payment takes place (if payment is a week in arrears, explain this clearly, possibly with an example)
- holiday pay details
- sick pay allowances
- pension scheme details if applicable
- period of notice required on either side
- probation period.

The Department of Trade and Industry has documents which will assist you in writing this contract, and they can be obtained from your JobCentre. They are PL700 and PL700A.

The probation period is one in which you have a chance to assess the employee and they, in turn, have a chance to decide if this is where they want to work. During any probation period, it is wise for the employer to meet with the employee to chart their progress or lack of it and to keep notes of the conversations. It is possible that this might be necessary if the employee does not meet the employer's expectations during this period.

Induction or orientation

When a new employee starts, there is likely to be an element of nervousness and so steps must be taken to alleviate this. In addition, the employee should be asked to start work at a time at which you or your spouse are available to carry out an effective induction process.

If you did not meet again with the employee after the interview, now is the time to complete the formality of the contract of employment. Once this is done, the employee should be introduced to any other staff members. Follow a process along the lines of the following:

- Show them where they leave their outdoor clothes – locker room or whatever.

- Show where the toilets are that they can use.

- Explain when and where meals and coffee breaks are taken if relevant.

- Walk them through the property inside and out.

- Give them a brochure if you have one and run through the relevant details so that they become familiar with the product.

- Explain the fire safety regulations and show the evacuation plan and the external meeting points. Bear in mind that guests will expect help from staff in case of emergency.

- Explain the general rules for lateness and call-in requirement in event of their sickness. This will help you in the future.

Training

All employees, irrespective of previous qualification, require an element of training in order to achieve the quality standards of the property. For experienced employees, the first few days will be an orientation to your standards and expectations, and at this time, you should try to obtain a commitment to these standards from the employees. One problem with hiring experienced staff is that they will do things the way they did them in their last employment, and if that standard is not your standard, then you have to retrain.

Key to this for you following the induction period, is to observe thoroughly during the first week or so and, in a positive way, explain where standards are not quite being met. The information approach is a better one than a 'get it right or else' one.

For new employees without previous experience, be aware that this will take additional time for the person who is carrying out the training. Training will slow down the process of getting the work done, but effective communication of procedures and standards at this stage will pay off through standards being achieved as part of normal working practices from the early days of the employee's time with you.

Ideally, anyone involved in training should attend an 'on-the-job trainer' course, which is likely to be offered by your local college or enterprise agency. If it is not possible to take this, consider the following steps to effective training:

- Show and tell, with emphasis on explaining the reason why things are done that way.

- Give the trainee the opportunity to practise while you watch, coaching and correcting in a positive way.

- As competency builds, reduce supervision but check back from time to time.

- When the task is carried out correctly, praise the employee.

Employee training can be followed up by the use of job aids which can be prepared by the owner and which might show diagrams of steps in making the bed for example, or might simply be a numbered step-by-step routine for cleaning a bathroom.

Performance appraisal

Although you are a small business, the feelings of staff are the same as those in a large corporation. They want to know how they are doing and if you, the employer, are satisfied with their work.

From time to time, perhaps twice a year, arrange to sit down with the employee and evaluate performance. It can sometimes help to go back to the job description and see if this has changed for the particular employee. Job descriptions are fluid documents and, sometimes, for a reason such as improved technology, a task might be eliminated and others taken on.

Start by putting the employee at ease and explaining that the aim of the process is to improve standards, if necessary, but also to air any issues that need to be aired. Start by picking on an outstanding area of the employee's performance. Thank them for that excellent aspect of the job. Now discuss any areas which may not be quite up to standard and ask the employee for any thoughts as to why they are not quite right. This may show a lack of understanding of what the standard is, and therefore this can be resolved amicably through further training. Occasionally, there may be disagreement on a particular standard and this now comes up for discussion. It may be that you can agree and change the standard, or that you have to explain more clearly the reason why that standard must remain, and why the employee must work to that standard. The interview ends when you summarise the meeting and the agreements reached regarding standards, and with thanks for the good work done.

On occasions, if you have a less than perfect employee, the process is important to establish levels of performance which must be reached. With this employee, it should be made clear that the standards that must be reached within a certain time period.

In both cases, notes to the file are made. Remember that employees have the right to see their file, so be factual and realistic on the notes you make.

Discipline

In a small operation, the discipline process is likely to be an informal one, in which as you see something happening which is not right, you talk about it there and then and hopefully resolve the issue. This has the benefit of not allowing molehills to become mountains, and in general is likely to eliminate long-term problems.

Where an employee is becoming a problem then a process must be used by which the employee is told of the issue and asked to make changes. This should be a 'positive discipline' process at the outset, in that the employee is shown how to get it right and then evaluated to see if change has taken place. If not, then the process becomes formal and follows a three-strike process with written warnings and then, as a last resort, dismissal.

Motivation of staff

Having just spoken about discipline, it seems right to discuss briefly the concept of staff motivation. From what we hear in the media from time to time, motivation in the larger companies is a problem to achieve and many consultants receive lots of reward for creating a well-motivated workforce. In reality, motivation comes from the top and, in your case, you create the motivation or otherwise.

What motivates employees?

There is a general feeling that employees work for money and money alone. However, without getting too academic, it is fair to say that while employees are concerned about earning a fair wage which will cover their basic needs, they want more from a job. Without spending too much time discussing the theories of Maslow, McClelland and even McGregor, it is safe to say that they would all agree that there are certain things that employees want from a job other than the wage packet.

They want:

- a pleasant work environment

- companionship and camaraderie

- to know what is going on

- to be in on things and feel good if they are involved in the decision-making process and to use their expertise

- recognition for the good work that they do. Ideally, verbal, and hopefully financial reward in the form of a bonus or extra payment.

In a small business, it is easier to achieve this by following a good induction and training process. In addition, by keeping communication processes open and being open and frank with employees, as well as giving good facilities and a happy environment, motivation can be achieved. Do not underestimate the importance of this for your employees and for your peace of mind.

> **Remember that a happy and motivated staff will reflect positively on the feeling your guests have when in your property.**

Health and safety issues

In Chapter 1, I mentioned the need for employer's liability insurance, which ensures you have insurance coverage in respect of injuries to employees. The relevant legislation is the Employer's Liability (Compulsory Insurance) Act 1969.

Other relevant legislation includes the Health and Safety at Work Act of 1974 and this presents the standards for health and safety of employees and customers. Under this act, if you decide to have employees, you are required to register with the Environmental Health Department of your local authority.

In *An Introduction To Health and Safety* provided by the Health and Safety Executive, there is a great deal of information which is relevant to small businesses. See the Appendix for the address and contact number.

This document helps in many areas of operation, some of which relate to the hospitality industry. Most importantly, it details what health and safety is all about and explains why there are health and safety laws. It also emphasises the fact that the laws apply to all businesses and explains who administers the law on behalf of the Health and Safety Executive. It explains the role of inspectors and how to contact an inspector in order to obtain information and it points out that there is a need to register a business as well as to have employer's liability insurance. In addition, it explains that certain health and safety posters need to be displayed in your property.

You are expected to provide employees with protective clothing if the employee, in the course of their job, handles harmful substances. This might relate in this industry to the use of certain cleaning materials.

Training should be given to employees who must handle and carry heavy items, possibly carrying guest luggage. Training should also be given to staff to be generally neat and tidy in their work to avoid the risk of other staff or even guests falling over something or tripping up. In our industry, vacuum cleaner cables are a source of many accidents.

You should prepare for your establishment some general guidelines or policy, which will become part of the induction process. Depending on the place of work of the employee it should cover the areas of danger they are likely to face or even cause. It should have guidelines for what to do in the case of an accident and should explain where first aid kits are located. It is the employer's responsibility to ensure the first aid kit is stocked at all times with relevant items. Many suppliers will contact you offering a variety of possible combinations of first aid kits, and this is not an area to scrimp and save. Purchase the best one you can.

The kitchen is a potential danger point and training should take place relevant to handling hot items and sharp items, as well as coping with the possibility of different types of fire, which require different treatments. Contact your local fire brigade who will from time to time assist you in carrying out staff training.

Risk assessment is required if you have five or more employees, and you are required to identify possible risk areas within your property, and show through your health and safety policy how to reduce or eliminate the risk if possible.

Payment of staff

No doubt you hope that your establishment will offer a motivational environment and that employees will enjoy working there. Initially however, the potential staff member applies without knowing about the way you run the property. They want a job and, at this stage, the wage offered is an issue. There is a National Minimum Wage Act 1998, as well as an Equal Pay Act 1970 which must be taken into consideration. The latter relates to issues concerning men and women having the same wage for the same job. You must comply, but more importantly, you must offer a wage which is competitive for the region and which will be of interest to the applicant.

In addition, National Insurance contributions must be made and tax paid. The Appendix gives numbers and websites for the relevant bodies. There is also a helpline for new employers.

It is likely that you will employ some part-time staff. If your property is seasonal, it may be convenient to hire students, preferably from a hospitality programme. There are regulations which relate to the employment of part-timers, and they should be treated no less favourably than full-timers. This includes pay, pensions, holidays, training and promotions. A helpline is shown in the Appendix.

Summary

Staffing should not simply be a 'hit or miss' activity, in which you trust to luck to hire the right employee. Remember that your property, your guests and your reputation are at risk when you take someone on. Set up an employment system that will find the best applicants. Develop an induction and training process relevant to the needs of your business, and follow it. Some time spent in setting up such a system will be of benefit to you and might well save you going through the recruitment process time after time.

The following are the action steps for Chapter 11:

♦ After a trial period make the decision as to whether you need staff, how many, and what roles they will fill in your hotel or guesthouse.

♦ Write brief job descriptions and job specifications.

♦ Make a decision on rates of pay after some investigation of local expectations.

♦ Decide the best place to advertise and write the advertisement.

♦ Plan the interview and the time to spend on the interview.

♦ Select the best employees.

♦ Plan an induction checklist and carry out good induction.

♦ Prepare a training plan in which you show and tell, and the employee practises the practical tasks.

♦ Give some thought to motivational techniques and how you will communicate with employees.

♦ Be sure to follow relevant employment legislation.

Appendix

Inland Revenue

Website for general help and advice	www.inlandrevenue.gov.uk
Helpline for newly self-employed	08459 154 515
Website for newly self-employed	www.inlandrevenue.gov.uk/startingup
New employers' helpline	0845 607 0143

National Insurance and other helplines

National Insurance contributions	0845 915 7141
National minimum wage	0845 6000 678
Part-time staff helpline	020 7215 5933
Pensions	0115 974 1777
Self-assessment	0845 9000 444
VAT Customs & Excise website	www.hmce.gov.uk
VAT	See local telephone book
Disability discrimination helpline	0345 622 633

Support for small businesses

Website for England	www.businessadviceonline.org

England Business Link   0845 604 5678

Website for Scotland   (Lowlands) www.sbgateway.com
Telephone for Lowlands   0845 609 6611

Website for Highlands and Islands   www.hie.co.uk
Highlands and Islands Enterprise   01463 715 400

Website for Wales   www.businessconnect.org.uk
Business Connect (Wales)   0845 796 9798

Website for Northern Ireland   www.ledu-ni.gov.uk

Local Enterprise Development (NI)   028 9019 1031

Small Business Service   www.businessadviceonline.org

Enterprise Investment Scheme   029 2032 7400

Help with computers & IT   0845 715 2000

Computer help website   www.ukonlineforbusiness.gov.uk

Federation of Small Businesses   www.fsb.org.uk

Other useful contacts

Environment Agency   0845 9333 111

Scottish Environmental Protection Agency   01786 457 700
SEPA website   www.sepa.org.uk

Northern Ireland   028 9054 0540
NI website   www.environment-agency.org.uk

Health & Safety   08701 545 500
Health & Safety website   www.hse.gov.uk/policy/webindex.htm

Health and Safety Executive   Information Centre
                                                        Broad Lane
                                                        Sheffield S3 7HQ.

Licences to Trade website   www.dag-business.gov.uk
British Chambers of Commerce   020 7565 2000

B.C. of C. website	www.britishchambers.org.uk
Association of Chartered Certified Accountants	020 7242 6855
ACCA website	www.acca.org.uk
Institute of Chartered Accountants	020 7920 8100
ICA website	www.icaew.co.uk
Institute of Chartered Accountants of Scotland	0131 225 5673
ICAS website	www.icas.org.uk
Food Hygiene Line	0845 608 6089
Website	www.food.gov.uk/cleanup
Office of Fair Trading	020 7211 8000
Website	www.oft.gov.uk
Independent Financial Advisers	0117 971 1177
Website	www.unbiased.co.uk
Council for Registered Gas Installers	0125 637 2200
CORGI website	www.corgi-gas.co.uk
The Office of Gas and Electricity Markets	020 7828 0898
Ofgem website	www.ofgem.gov.uk
Office of Telecommunication	020 7634 8700
OFTEL website	www.oftel.gov.uk
Office of Water Services	0121 625 1300
OFWAT website	www.open.gov.uk/ofwat/
Fax Preference Service	020 7291 3330
(Eliminate unwanted Fax messages)	www.fpsonline.org.uk
Performing Rights Society	0800 0684828
Website	www.prs.co.uk
Phonographic Performances Ltd.	020 7534 1000
Website	www.ppluk.com

Hotel Industry Associations

British Hospitality Association	020 7404 7744
BHA website	www.bha-online.org.uk
National Council of Hotel Associations	0122 583 5088
NCHA website	www.bed-and-breakfast.org
Hotel & Catering International Management Association	020 8661 4900
HCIMA website	www.hcima.org.uk
British Institute of Innkeeping	0127 668 4449
BII website	www.barzone.co.uk
Hospitality Training Foundation	020 8579 2400
HTF website	www.htf.org.uk
The Restaurant Association	020 7831 8727
Website	www.ragb.co.uk
National Council of Hotel Associations	0122 583 5088
NCHA website	www.bed-and-breakfast.org

Software System Contacts

Sage Software	www.sage.co.uk
QuickBooks	www.quickbooks.co.uk
Dosh	www.dosh.co.uk
Clearly Business	www.clearlybusiness.com

Tourist Boards

English Tourist Board	020 8563 0302
ETB website	www.englishtourism.org.uk

VisitScotland	0131 332 2433
VisitScotland website	www.visitscotland.com
	also www.scotexchange.net
Wales	029 2049 9909
Wales website	www.wales-tourist-board.gov.uk
Northern Ireland	01232 231221
NI website	www.ni-tourism.com

National hotel sales agents

Robert Barry & Co	020 7344 6666
Milner House	www.robertbarry.co.uk
14 Manchester Square	
London W1U 3PP.	(Branches throughout UK)
Christie & Co	020 7227 0700
Website	www.christies.com
Bruce & Co. (Scotland)	0131 477 6060
Website	www.bruceandco.co.uk
Bruce & Company	0193 547 3878
Website	www.bruceandcompany.co.uk

Most national agents advertise in the *Caterer and Hotelkeeper*. This can be purchased weekly from most newsagent's. The address of this magazine is:

Caterer and Hotelkeeper	020 8652 3221
Reed Business Information	www.caterer.com
Quadrant House	
The Quadrant	
Sutton	
Surrey SM2 5AS.	

Helpful How To Books

Buying and Running a Small Hotel, Ken Parker.

Starting and Running a B&B, Stewart Whyte, Nigel Jess.

Preparing A Winning Business Plan, Mathew Record.

Book-Keeping and Accounting for the Small Business, Peter Taylor.

Starting Your Own Business, Jim Green.

Deliver Outstanding Customer Service, Susan and Derek Nash.

Start & Run Your Own Business, Alan Le Marinel

Index